ABANDON SHIP!

ABANDON SHIP!

*The Post-War Memoirs of
Captain Tony McCrum RN*

TONY McCRUM

Pen & Sword
MARITIME

First published in Great Britain in 2012 by
PEN & SWORD MARITIME
An imprint of
Pen & Sword Books Ltd
47 Church Street
Barnsley
South Yorkshire
S70 2AS

ISBN 978 1 84884 666 1

A CIP catalogue record for this book is
available from the British Library

Typeset in Ehrhardt
by Chic Media Ltd

Printed and bound in England by MPG

Pen & Sword Books Ltd incorporates the Imprints of Pen & Sword Aviation,
Pen & Sword Family History, Pen & Sword Maritime, Pen & Sword Military,
Pen & Sword Discovery, Wharncliffe Local History, Wharncliffe True Crime,
Wharncliffe Transport, Pen & Sword Select, Pen & Sword Military Classics,
Leo Cooper, The Praetorian Press, Remember When,
Seaforth Publishing and Frontline Publishing

For a complete list of Pen & Sword titles please contact
PEN & SWORD BOOKS LIMITED
47 Church Street, Barnsley, South Yorkshire, S70 2AS, England
E-mail: enquiries@pen-and-sword.co.uk
Website: www.pen-and-sword.co.uk

Contents

Dedication

To the memory of Angela

Chapter 1

Homecoming

I'm alive, I'm alive, I'm alive! The thought kept drumming into me again and again, not because of an escape from some dramatic accident, but because the end of the Second World War had suddenly and unexpectedly been announced on the radio. It was 15 August 1945. Fear of death and perils of war had vanished and I had survived.

On 6 and 9 August respectively, two atom bombs had destroyed the Japanese cities of Hiroshima and Nagasaki. Nuclear war had been launched and, on the 15th, the Emperor of Japan had ordered all of his forces to surrender to the nearest Allied commander. History had been made.

Now, in October, I was on my way home in HMS *Tartar*, a vessel of the 8th Destroyer Squadron, which had been part of the mighty British Eastern Fleet based in Trincomalee in Ceylon (now Sri Lanka), where we had been preparing for an incredibly tricky invasion of Malaya in the autumn. We were steaming happily homewards, longing to be reunited with our families. It was a glorious end to six years of bitter struggle. We were victorious, euphoric and relieved.

I, Lieutenant Tony McCrum, aged twenty-six, had been on board for the past year as the Staff Signal Officer to the Squadron Commander, Basil Jones, a genial, enjoyable boss who was a fine naval warrior with a great fighting record in the English Channel, where the squadron had sunk a number of German warships in 1944.

It was a strange feeling to be steaming along rather slowly because we now had to economise on fuel. We lacked the spice of ginger that kept us on high alert in wartime when we had raced along at 20 knots or more; the converse was that we had complete security.

ABANDON SHIP!

The peace took some getting used to. Was it really all over?

Colombo, Aden, Port Said, Malta, Gibraltar ... and sight of the Cornish coast. At last, *Tartar* entered Plymouth Sound, one of the most beautiful harbours in Britain, a vast expanse of water framed by the Cornish cliffs and coves to the west and the stark Devon headland to the east, with the city of Plymouth stretching along its northern shore. Beyond the city, far off on the skyline, I could see the granite tors of Dartmoor near my home and they reminded me of glorious days of hillwalking in peacetime and the solitude of those wild moors.

It was late in the afternoon on a cheerless November day, but our families were waiting on the jetty and it could have been snowing a blizzard for all we cared. At last we were home.

At Devil's Point, below which Plymouth Sound turns into the river Tamar, we were given a cheer from a welcoming crowd standing round the memorial to Captain Scott of Antarctic fame. There to welcome me was my mother and my brother, Michael, recently a sub-lieutenant in the Royal Naval Volunteer Reserve who had been flown home early from the British Pacific Fleet so that he could start the autumn term at Cambridge University. He had been a survivor of a double kamikaze suicide attack on his ship, the aircraft carrier HMS *Victorious*. The ship had been badly damaged but, fortunately, my brother, who was on the bridge at the time, was unscathed. We were a lucky family. Father, uncle, brother and self – all serving in the Navy – had survived the war without even a scratch.

Throughout the war my mother had looked after my youngest brother, now seventeen and a naval cadet, on her own, while her two older sons were at sea and writing home infrequently. She must have had many bleak moments worrying about us. The war was perhaps far harder for those left behind and always dreading the worst, whereas we had the adrenalin and excitement to keep us going. Since my father's desertion of my mother and his three sons ten years earlier he had played no part in our upbringing and my mother had sole responsibility for looking after us. Also, for several years she looked after her sister's four children when my aunt was marooned in India. Somehow, through all those years of travail she managed to maintain a normal life for us and never showed her misery. She may not have been a successful career woman but she was a great lady.

Standing on the bridge as we wended our way across Plymouth Sound and up the river Tamar, many thoughts flashed through my mind. It was difficult to believe that this really was the end of the war and that we would not be sailing out again tomorrow to fight U-boats in the Atlantic. I had witnessed amazing acts of courage, such as that of Leading Seaman Macleod, a Hebridean fisherman in peacetime, who had continued firing his anti-aircraft Oerlikon gun as the water lapped at his feet in the sinking ship HMS *Skipjack* at Dunkirk. I had watched soldiers storming ashore in the face of heavy enemy fire at Salerno. I had served with men and women who discovered resources in themselves that they did not know they had and with people of all ranks who, faced with danger, found they were capable of performing extraordinary deeds of courage and endurance. Many discovered that they had an unexpected strength of character, which would give them a confidence that would last them a lifetime.

For those who had survived the war, whole in body and mind, it had been a galvanising experience, but not for those whose bodies or spirit were maimed, and there were many others who never came back. As we, the lucky ones, prepared to be reunited with our families, there were many whose memories were bleak.

After picking up our moorings in the Hamoaze, the families came off by boat and headed up the gangway for a very public reunion on deck: a peck on the cheek for my mother and a nodding smile for my brother. Terribly British. We drank to everlasting peace, and that was that.

Chapter 2

Sea Change

After the joy and excitement of homecoming there was a strange sense of emptiness. Life seemed flat and unemotional, and the end of the war unnatural. We had been fighting for so long that it had become an almost normal way of life and it was difficult to remember what peacetime was like. For six years we had lived on a precipice of terror mixed with excitement and exhilaration. When the terrors passed there was the intense relief of having survived and the euphoria that followed.

At sea, day had followed day, more often than not with no action or excitement, then an occasional spasm of fear, but so seldom and so brief that it left no scars. Gradually I had come to accept this rollercoaster life between boredom and excitement as normal. I suppose we had geared ourselves up to not thinking about the downside of war, the drowning, the maiming, the mental stress and illness. I didn't waste time worrying about such fears – fears that I kept locked away in some deep cellar within my brain. Only very occasionally, during a particularly unpleasant episode, did these spectres rise up and assault one's morale, but they soon dissolved and life resumed its carefully balanced path.

Throughout the war I was dogged by the dread that I might reveal the germ of fear that nestled deep down within me and might expose me to cowardice. As a result of the terrible slaughter on the Western Front in the First World War I had always been bitterly opposed to war when I was growing up, but I had no doubts that *our* war was absolutely justified. I had been willing to make any sacrifice to defeat the terrible Nazi evil. Truly, it was a Just War, and somehow, I got through.

After the welcome home, most of us went on leave. For me it was an intense joy to see the granite tors standing proud on the hilltops of Dartmoor and the deep valleys, unchanged for thousands of years, reminding me of more lasting values. Belstone, our little moorland village above the valley of the river Taw, had been untouched by the war.

Soon I came down to earth with a bump and found myself as Duty Officer with a skeleton crew on board *Tartar* in the bottom of a dry dock in Devonport Dockyard. The destroyer was being paid off. It was sad to see this ocean greyhound squatting on the chocks in a filthy dock surrounded by the splattered wrecks of dockyard buildings. The dockyard had been heavily bombed in the Plymouth blitz and central Plymouth was a sea of rubble, flattened as far as the eye could see.

People looked grey and miserable for good reason. Rationing of every kind was even more severe than it had been in wartime. Even bread, never rationed in war, was scarce. Wedding dresses had to be made out of curtains, or parachutes, if your fiancé was in the RAF. There was a hideous choice of furniture, known as Utility furniture, which was also rationed. Somehow people had felt that when the war ended there would be a sudden cornucopia of plenty, but it was going to be a long time before the flow of food increased. The Dutch and other people in many central European countries were literally starving and we were foregoing our rations to save them from disaster. The RAF was parachuting food supplies into Holland, where the food shortage was at its worst.

People were exhausted after their wartime efforts. It was an anti-climax and we had to adjust to a bleak, chilly West Country winter and this unexpectedly drab world of austerity. For six years everyone had been wound up, ready to face danger, but now the scent of peril and the fear of death were gone. The absence of these wartime challenges made life seem rather dull. This may sound as if I thought war was enjoyable, which it most certainly wasn't, but it had been galvanising.

There was, of course, a counterpoint; we could sleep in peace. But there were deep feelings of guilt. Why had I survived when so many others had died? I remembered with sadness the many good friends who had perished. Whether or not you lived or died seemed to have been a lottery.

These introspective musings didn't last long and I decided it was time to enjoy life to the full and forget the miseries. Having survived the war one might as well relish the pleasures of life. To hell with the gloom, I thought; we're only young once, bring on the dancing girls. I was only twenty-seven, my life had been on hold for six years and I had much time to make up. In naval terms, it was a time for 'letting go the end,' an expression harking back to the days of sail, describing the moment after sailors had been hauling on a rope with a heavy load on the end; task completed, they'd drop the rope on the deck and 'let go the end', heaving a sigh of relief. In modern times, it had become an expression for letting go all restraints and having a wonderful party, relationship, experience or 'whatever takes yer fancy.'

My time in the bottom of a dry dock soon ended and from being a staff officer to a warrior captain who had long departed and responsible for the communications of six destroyers, I was whisked away to a hutted camp on the outskirts of Plymouth, where the Devonport Naval Signal School languished. The camp consisted of Nissen huts in a dank and dripping wood above the banks of the river Plym. Pre-war it had been a holiday camp for naturists, otherwise known as nudists. They had apparently been free to wander around in this leafy environment stark naked, although the locals said that, due to the thickness of the vegetation, it was almost impossible to catch a glimpse of a glorious body.

The Signal School trained junior ratings (sailors) for the next step up the rungs of the lower deck ladder – short courses on radio and teleprinter operating and visual signalling with flags, semaphore and flashing lamps. I was to be the senior instructor, responsible for the standards set and for the performance of the instructors. After my days of standing on the bridge of a destroyer steaming at 25 knots and screening a huge fleet of battleships and aircraft carriers in the Bay of Bengal, this was a trifle tame.

Apart from these instructional courses the main function of the camp was as a holding depot for sailors being demobilised, as was happening to all the wartime conscripts. When their great day came they were issued with demob suit, trilby hat, and matching shoes and socks and they bade farewell to the Navy from the back of a departing lorry, giving three hearty cheers as they cleared the sentry on the gate for the last time.

This regular routine of demobbing produced a slap-happy atmosphere amongst both officers and ratings as they waited for their release dates. Being a career officer, I was in the Navy for life. Discipline at this time was lax and there was no enthusiasm for new ideas, least of all from the Captain, who was an alcoholic. It was a world apart from being on a ship at sea. The only bright spots were my two assistants, Len Hubbard and Fred Tarling, nuggets of gold, men from the lower deck who had risen to a single-stripe commission as commissioned signal boatswains – a lovely title. They kept me sane, and Fred remained a personal friend until his death many years later.

On my first day Len Hubbard introduced me to my office.

'It's a bit small and I'm afraid there's no telephone.'

'No telephone?' I exclaimed. 'How can I possibly do my job without a phone?'

'Telephones are rationed and Miss Long says you will have to wait your turn.'

'Who is this Miss Long?' I asked.

'She is the Assistant to the Command Signal Officer and the Queen of all Telephones.'

Oh! One of these bloody Wren[1] officers who has spent the war at home in a cushy shore job, I thought.

After the end of the war telephone lines were severely rationed and allocated mainly by rank; a self-important lieutenant was at the tail end of the queue. But I wasn't going to put up with it.

I told Len Hubbard, 'Get Miss Long on the communal phone and I'll soon sort her out.'

Miss Long rang me back. I demanded my telephone and conveyed to her that I was exceedingly important and could not do my job without one.

She had a nice voice and hit my request for six.

'You'll get a telephone when your name comes up to the top of the list. There is no way you can jump the queue. Goodbye.'

Len Hubbard poked his head round the door.

'Any luck with the lovely Miss Long?'

'Go away,' I shouted.

The balloon of my self-esteem had been well and truly pricked. Some years later, Miss Long became Mrs McCrum, and we lived happily ever after.

This was the beginning of a dreary, aimless winter. One consolation in these lacklustre months was my home on Dartmoor, easily accessible on weekends, and I was able to climb the hills again and walk off on my own for a day to ponder the mysteries of life.

Back at the Signal School we turned to partying to relieve the boredom. There was much drinking and, because there were no drink-driving laws, we rocked around the country pubs, carried by my self-drive naval car that allowed me precious, unrationed petrol, which was like gold dust at that time.

How come I had the benefit of this luxury at a time when private cars were almost unobtainable? I had picked up a part-time second job as Command Signal Officer for the Plymouth Command, which took me all of two days a week. On those days I retreated to the underground bunker in Plymouth, where the wartime headquarters was buried deep under the rocks of the coastline. This was a caretaker job as most of the wartime command signals organisations were being dismantled, but I needed a car to visit the remaining signal and radio stations in the command. Some relic of a wartime order that had never been rescinded allowed a limited amount of private use of such official vehicles.

When I first moved into the Command Signal Officer's underground office I was slightly dismayed to find a young Wren officer sitting behind a glass partition in an annexe to my office. This was the dreaded Miss Long. For those two days a week she was my assistant, efficient and charming, displaying no hard feelings over my rudeness about the telephone.

Still feeling the bruises of my last wartime relationship, I maintained a friendly working partnership with Miss Long. She didn't stay long though, as she was made redundant, and I was sad to see her go.

I settled into this unstrenuous life, which seemed to have little purpose except to enjoy myself and make up for six wasted years. I said 'Yes' to every invitation and was somewhat surprised when I arrived at the home of one very brief and recent girlfriend to be handed a rake and shears and was expected to set-to with four other young men to clear an overgrown shrubbery. The young lady's father was a captain RN, so we got stuck in with gusto, if a trifle unwillingly. It was a clever move by the father, who had three nubile daughters ripe for engagement. To be fair, when we had finished the job we were given an excellent lunch and plenty of beer to slake our thirsts, but I didn't jump that particular fence.

This was typical of life in 1946 – fleeting relationships and no permanent entanglements. I didn't want to settle down. Settling down meant weddings, home every evening, screaming babies, nappies and sleepless nights. That could all keep for later.

If existence in Britain was depressing, it was far worse in Europe. The Germans suffered hideously; perhaps some of them deserved it. The Russians refused to release their German prisoners of war, who were incarcerated in terrible conditions in Siberian Gulags, where many died, and the survivors were not repatriated until 1956 – eleven years after the end of the war.

At home, the Labour Government, voted in by a huge majority (including my vote) in 1945, was in power, committed to old fashioned socialism. They nationalised the coal mines, the railways, the buses, the ports, the Bank of England and many other firms. They introduced the National Health Service and a comprehensive welfare system. Despite the austerity, there was hope that things would get better.

My work in the Signal School needed no over-exertion. I became used to the relaxed atmosphere in the camp and knew how to keep my regularly half-pissed captain off my back. We were coasting. Into this lackadaisical world, a bomb burst.

SEA CHANGE

'Message for you, Sir, from Admiral Pridham-Wippell. He will see you in his office at 1100 hours tomorrow, Friday, at Mount Wise, Plymouth.'

'What have you done, Sir?' asked Len Hubbard.

What had I done? My mind raced back to see what crime might have merited this encounter with the all-highest, for Admiral Pridham-Wippell was Commander-in-Chief, Plymouth Command, just one below God.

In fear and trembling I presented myself in his office the next day, expecting execution. I stood smartly to attention in front of his desk. What looked to me like an extremely ancient man looked up.

'I am changing my flag lieutenant [I had heard on the grapevine that he had just sacked him]. People tell me you might do.'

I didn't feel called upon to comment.

'Go away and come back tomorrow and tell me if you accept the job.'

About turn, quick march.

Oh lord! What had I done to deserve this? This would mean a complete change in my lifestyle. From an easy-going life with my own age group and no one to bother me I was to be shunted into a world of the strictest protocol and tied to an old man. I would have to live in Admiralty House, the Commander-in-Chief's official residence, with him and his chief of staff.

A flag lieutenant has little time for himself and waits upon his boss's wishes and orders twenty-four hours a day. He organises his programme, gets him to the right place at the right time and in the correct uniform and spends much of his time helping to entertain senior officers, civic leaders and local bigwigs. In the Navy he is known colloquially as a 'flunkey', which the dictionary describes as a 'male servant, a footman, a lackey, often used contemptuously.' One mistake at a dinner party can cause mayhem. If he places Mrs Town Clerk in the wrong order of seniority at the dinner table, the town hall erupts. It was not really my cup of tea. A walk with my dog on Dartmoor and a packet of sandwiches for lunch was more my line.

What was I to do? It was undoubtedly a feather in my cap and it would be a unique opportunity to see how the Navy was run from the top. My friends in the camp were of no help.

11

'Tony, you dress like a scran bag. Your clothes are a disgrace; you can't even play bridge. You won't last a week.'

'Thanks everybody. I'll make my own mind up.'

It would be good for me to get into the limelight as I was rather inclined to fade into the background whenever I could. I had never mixed with such senior officers before and I was inclined to be overly critical of top brass. I wondered how my left-wing views would coexist with the grand life and I thought long and hard about my decision. Looking back, I don't know why I made such a meal of it, but it was typical of many of the decisions I have made throughout my life. I often felt torn between two forces: the easy life or the challenge of the unknown path? Was it in the genes I inherited or was it just me?

On my mother's side of the family there was a string of stern naval officers. Her grandfather was an admiral and his brother a captain lost at sea off Memel in 1853 during the Baltic War against Russia. There was even an ancestor who was a captain who had fought under Nelson. So there they all were, looking over my shoulder.

My father's family came from a lowly background as smallholders in County Monaghan in Ireland – a few pigs, a cow and some hens clucking around in a muddy yard. From these humble beginnings there emerged a string of entrepreneurs who became successful manufacturers of linen.

It was my great-great-grandfather McCrum who made the breakthrough. He lived in a small cottage on the banks of the river Callan, 2 miles south of Armagh, and he was clever enough to realise that running water meant power, so he built a mill and started manufacturing linen. He expanded and his business prospered, and his son, my great-grandfather, enlarged it and made oodles of cash. Within two generations, the McCrums had become rather grand and great-grandfather built a mansion on the site of his father's cottage, which I had visited when I was four. For some extraordinary reason, this vast mansion was always called 'The Cottage'.

Originally, the family were strict Presbyterians, which I suspect planted that anti-authoritarian streak in me. As the family became more prosperous they adopted the trappings of gentry and converted to the Anglican Church, the Church of Ireland, but remained strongly teetotal. Then, my grandfather reversed the process and gambled away the family fortunes. He kicked over all the hardworking traces of his forebears and spent the winters in the casinos of Monte Carlo. He married a lively Canadian lady for a short spell, begat one son, my father, then left his wife and never remarried. But he redeemed himself in the eyes of my grandchildren by inventing the penalty kick in football in 1890 and, after a long battle with the national and international football authorities, he got it adopted worldwide. His rules live on to this day.

Standing in front of the Admiral's desk next day, I said, 'Yes, Sir,' and a starting date was agreed.

Notes

1. The term Wren describes female officers and ratings of the Women's Royal Naval Service and was commonly used throughout the Navy. The correct abbreviation is WRNS, the Women's Royal Naval Service.

Chapter 3

The Flunkey

For me the move from the easygoing life at the Signal School to the imposing Commander-in-Chief's residence was a transformation to the high life such as I had never sampled before. Mount Wise House was a beautiful Georgian residence with eight bedrooms, a ballroom, a drawing room looking straight across Plymouth Sound to Mount Edgcumbe Woods, and a dining room to seat thirty. It was a treasure and I soon got used to living in such splendour, despite my egalitarian views.

I had a personal Jeeves, a naval steward, to keep me looking smart. I had to look posh now at all times, which was not my natural inclination. On my first morning he called me and began removing all my clothes.

'Hey, I'm just going to get dressed,' I called out.

'Sir,' he said, 'shirts and underwear are worn clean every day in Admiralty House and the underwear must be ironed so that it is warm to the skin.'

Crikey. He didn't know I only had three sets of pants and vests – one on, one in the wash and only one spare – and they would not stand up to this routine. So I quickly had to buy some more before my Jeeves found me out.

On the job I always had to look smart and even in plain clothes I always wore a suit. In the evenings we always dressed for dinner: bum-freezer jacket, bow tie and evening shirt. (A bum-freezer is a jacket cut away above the buttocks, hence causing the bum to chill.) Whenever on duty with the Admiral I had to wear gold lace aiguillettes, which hung down over my chest and looked rather like gold-plated lavatory chains. Aiguillettes were supposed to represent the pegs and halter with which an aide-de-camp tethered the general's horse. I can't think why the Navy copied it. There weren't many horses in ships at sea.

Admiral Pridham-Wippell turned out to be a very nice man who had been wounded during the war and had undiagnosed lung cancer due to inhaling oil fuel in the sea when he had had to swim when HMS *Barham* blew up after being torpedoed by an Italian submarine. The cancer killed him shortly after he retired. In repose his face was rather severe, creased like a Brazil nut, but when he laughed a great light shone across it and he had a wicked twinkle in his eyes. He was as thin as a scarecrow, the early effects of his illness, probably. Not a tall man but when he stood up he was ramrod straight and could put the fear of the Almighty into a wayward officer.

Much of my time was taken up with social events as the Admiral was expected to entertain and this usually meant formal dinners. Then my job was to send out all the invitations and list the guests in their order of seniority and prepare a table plan in strict order of precedence. In my office there was a large leather-bound book going back to the 1850s, which recorded every official dinner party at Admiralty House: what was eaten, the wines, who the guests were and what the occasion was, plus the occasional scabrous comment about the guests by the flag lieutenant of the day. This 'bible' always had to be consulted to ensure that no one ate the same food twice. I would then discuss the plan with the Admiral, who might make some changes, but we were circumscribed by the British concern for the correct pecking order.

At the appointed time I would meet the guests at the front door, rather like a superior butler, and escort them to the Admiral and introduce them properly: 'The Earl and Countess of Mount Edgcumbe, Sir.' 'The Town Clerk and Mrs Entwhistle, Sir.' Once they had all arrived I had to make sure the stewards plied them with drinks and that no one was ever left out in the cold.

When the meal was ready the chief steward would throw open the double doors into the dining room and announce: 'Dinner is served, Sir,' and the guests then trooped in, in order of seniority. They would have been shown the seating plan while drinking and I hoped they would remember where to sit. With the first course the Admiral would talk to the lady on his right (the principal guest's wife) and the rest of us were supposed to follow suit and converse to our right – rather different to the shouting matches round our table at home in Belstone. Then the Admiral would switch to the lady on his left and we would all try to follow. This rather starchy routine did ensure that no one was left staring into outer space. An exception to this rule was when Lady Astor, the first woman MP and an American, came to lunch. She represented one of the Plymouth constituencies. She never drew breath and was wont to address the whole table as if it was a political meeting. She was most entertaining but no one else got a look-in. While this sounds very formal and heavy-going, the Admiral usually succeeded in making his parties a lot of fun.

After dinner he insisted on playing games, which some of the more pompous guests did not relish. One particular commodore's wife could always be relied upon to flutter the dovecotes of propriety. Leonie Raw was a Canadian who couldn't care tuppence for naval protocol and the Admiral knew that her party trick was to stand on her head. Ladies attending formal dinners did not normally stand on their heads. They always wore long skirts, so how could she decently stand on her head, as her skirt would end up all over her face, revealing her nether garments, if she had any? She neatly tucked the bottom of her skirt between her ankles, bent down to the floor, elegantly raised her legs straight above her head and remained immobile for some time, keeping her skirt firmly anchored. It was most graceful.

'Anyone else like to have a go?' said the Admiral, but there were never any takers.

Despite some tedious parties the job was an amazing experience. It was a hectic social life, which I had not met before. The chief of staff and I looked after the Admiral, and to prepare for these events we had a chief steward, an assistant chief steward, head chef, assistant chef and three stewards. There were also two gardeners, and for boating there was the Commander-in-Chief's barge and its crew. We weren't short of help.

Life wasn't just a long run of entertaining. The Admiral paid visits to ships when they came into harbour and, occasionally, we drove around to visit other naval places up and down the west coast.

Attending on the Admiral and living in the same house greatly curtailed my own social life. Just across the road from Admiralty House was the nest where the Wren officers lived and if I had a free moment I slipped over there for an evening amongst the young ladies. My future wife was amongst them but she was posted to Malta soon after I arrived and no spark was struck.

I was rather taken by surprise when my boss told me: 'My daughter, Heather, is coming to live with us for a while.' I didn't know he had any children but I was aware that he had been separated from his wife for a long time. Alarm bells rang in my mind. It was not unknown for admirals to expect that their flag lieutenants might marry their daughters, or at least one of them.

Heather arrived, rather a sad-faced young woman in her early twenties, pale and emaciated. She was charming and I think she had had a disturbed upbringing with a separated mother and father. I had some sympathy for her as my life had been disrupted by the desertion of my father, but we didn't form any serious bond. I did at least try to entertain her but this sometimes ended in disaster.

The Admiral had a smart gig with a blue enamelled hull with sails and oars but no engine. He hardly ever used it.

'Would it be all right, Sir, if I took the gig for a sailing picnic with Heather and a few friends? Just in the Sound: we won't go outside the breakwater.'

'Certainly,' he replied. 'Do you want any of the barge's crew to assist you?'

'No, thank you, Sir, we'll manage.'

With some friends of mine and Heather's we set off one afternoon, laden with picnic food provided by the Admiral's chef and booze provided by me. A delightful sail took us to a secluded cove on the Cornish coast and we ran the gig onto the beach so that the girls could get ashore dry-shod. There we had a jolly picnic. It was a fine evening and we played some light-hearted games. Nothing our mothers wouldn't have approved of. We lost count of the time. The stars came out and, as the leader, I thought it was time to head for home.

THE FLUNKEY

For a naval officer to forget the effect of tides is an unpardonable offence and also the height of stupidity, and that was exactly what I had done, lured into forgetfulness by the gin and tonics and my lovely companions. The gig, which was almost a sacred artefact, with the Admiral's flag painted on the bows, was high and dry, at least 20 feet from the nearest water. We tried to lift it to carry it to the water's edge but we were hopelessly uncoordinated. There was only one course of action; to wait for the tide to come in. I was not top of the pops with the guests and only Heather supported me.

'I'll tell Dad it wasn't really your fault.'

He wouldn't be fooled. So we waited and waited. At least it sobered us up and it was a beautiful night. Some three hours later we floated the gig off and sailed back.

'I hear you were rather late getting back,' is all that the Admiral said and he didn't let on whether he knew what had happened.

The year 1947 was the coldest winter in the West Country for many years. In my home village on Dartmoor the snow was up to the top of the hedges but in Admiralty House we were cosseted from the misery of a freezing cold, post-war winter. Overseas, the Empire was beginning to dissolve. India, Pakistan and Burma all became independent. The Royal Navy, which had ruled the seven seas, was being rapidly run down and long lines of mothballed warships were a common sight in British ports. Europe was still malnourished and struggling to recover from the war. The Russians effectively controlled Poland, Romania, Bulgaria, Hungary, Czechoslovakia, Yugoslavia, East Germany and the Baltic States and were bent on what Churchill described as 'indefinite expansion'. The year before, he had made his famous Iron Curtain speech: 'From Stettin on the Baltic to Trieste in the Adriatic an Iron Curtain has descended across the Continent.'

Many now prefer to forget that he also, in 1946, appealed for 'a kind of United States of Europe', a forerunner of the European Union. The end of the Second World War had not produced the easy peace that we all craved.

Just over a year of my gilded existence was coming to an end and I was mightily relieved. Despite my pleasant boss, I was not cut out for the life of a flunkey. I would much rather have been at sea, where I would be gaining useful seagoing experience. Nevertheless, I had observed the ways of senior naval officers and had socialised with the aristocracy and City bigwigs. I had learned how to act posh and how to entertain the nobs.

I was sad to say goodbye to my admiral and many of his staff, but I knew he was longing to set up home with the lady he loved. I had become aware that he had a special lady friend whom he had wanted to marry for many years but he never spoke about it. I only discovered the liaison because I had to check all the Admiralty House telephone bills and every morning before breakfast the Admiral called the same number and on the rare occasion that she came to stay, the calls ceased. She was a delightful lady and I thought it was so sad that he had had to wait so long to live with her because his long-estranged wife refused to grant him a divorce due to her strenuous religious convictions. At that time, I believe, both parties had to agree to a divorce. So if one party refused, it was a no-go. I believe the Admiral felt that as long as he was still serving the King, he could not take a live-in mistress. Before he drove away into retirement, I knew that, at last, he was going to be able to share a home with the lady he loved. How many would have had such a conception of honour in the twenty-first century?

The sad end to his personal dilemma was that both of them died within eighteen months of setting up home together.

I had no entanglements and went to my home on Dartmoor to await my next appointment.

Chapter 4

Seagoing Flunkey

Having said goodbye to Plymouth I wondered what those who must be obeyed had in store for me. Civilians imagine that one naval job is much the same as any other; in reality, the variety is huge. For the past two years I had spent most of my time as a typical social butterfly, a flunkey attending on my admiral, divorced from my equals and probably getting above my station. I had missed the seagoing experience, the cheerful badinage of sailors in small ships and the camaraderie of officers in the wardroom. I felt out of touch with the real navy.

So I hoped for an appointment to a seagoing ship as a commanding officer or another communications specialist sea appointment. Although I had been conscripted into the signals specialisation I was still first and foremost a seaman. In the Navy, unlike the Army, the specialists retained their basic seaman background and moved in and out of their specialism. My hope now was to move out again into the more open seas. There is something unique about 'being all of one company' in a small ship like a destroyer, which is the equivalent of the frigates in Nelson's day.

I desperately wanted to go 'down to the seas again, to the lonely sea and the sky', and all I asked for was 'a tall ship and a star to steer her by, and the grey mist on the sea's face, and a grey dawn breaking …' (*Sea Fever*, John Masefield), except I prefer a pink dawn and a ruddy-faced sun rising out of a clear horizon.

What did I get? Another flunkey's job, dressed up to look more attractive as Flag Lieutenant to the Commander-in-Chief, Home Fleet and Deputy Fleet Communications Officer. The latter part of the appointment didn't fool me. Deputies seldom get to exercise their role and the fleet communications officer is not likely to encourage any competition from another aspiring signal officer. I was to be a flunkey, yet again, gaining no real hands-on seagoing experience. I was most disappointed not to get a small ship command or a specialist signals appointment at sea.

Why had fate called me for this job? My new boss was Admiral Sir Rhoderick McGrigor, on whose staff I had briefly served as a lowly signal officer when he commanded Force H in the invasion of Sicily in 1943. Then I had seldom had any personal contact with him as my boss, the Squadron Signal Officer came between me and the Admiral, but I had been noticed as he recommended me 'to be mentioned in despatches,' which is the lowest of the decorations. Of course, it would be interesting to observe how an admiral commanded one of the major British fleets, the Home Fleet, the same as I had joined as a midshipman in HMS *Royal Oak* in 1936. It was much diminished now, reflecting the decline of the Royal Navy and the rundown of the British Empire. In 1936, the fleet consisted of six battleships, two aircraft carriers, five cruisers and twenty-four destroyers. This had now sunk to two battleships, two, sometimes three, aircraft carriers, three cruisers and eight destroyers.

Rhoddy McGrigor was one of the cleverest officers in the Navy but he didn't parade it. He had no pretensions and, unlike some senior officers, he was modest and reserved and commanded effortlessly without any bombast. He looked like a baby monkey with a long oval face and a huge head set upon a somewhat inadequately undersized body. He was a man of simple tastes, careful with his money, as a good Scot should be. He was kind and likeable and it was a privilege to serve him, but it was not the job I wanted.

Rhoddy had married late in life and had no children of his own. His wife was charming and a complete opposite; openhearted and delightfully scatty. They had adopted two little boys, children of a naval officer friend killed during the war. I believe their mother may also have been killed in an air raid but he never spoke about the children's background.

In December 1947, on a chilly, drizzly day, I attended the Admiral as he boarded his flagship, the battleship HMS *Duke of York*, in Portsmouth. The massed Royal Marine buglers sounded off the 'alert' to tell the world that the new commander-in-chief was arriving as he walked up the gangway, with me trailing behind, and was met by his predecessor, Admiral Syfret. There followed the traditional welcome to a commander-in-chief. The Royal Marine Band played *Rule Britannia* with gusto while we all stood to attention. I wondered whether Britannia did still rule the waves. The guard was inspected by the new boss and the two admirals went below for a brief chat. Presumably the outgoing admiral said, 'It's all yours now,' but there was no formal handing over of the baton and the departing admiral soon left by car.

Where was the rest of the fleet? Marooned alongside jetties in Plymouth, Portsmouth and Chatham. The years 1947 and 1948 were terrible for the Navy as shortages of every kind persisted in the country. There was a fuel crisis and not enough oil for the fleet to go to sea. Every ship in the Home Fleet was tied up to a jetty like beached whales and the Admiral had to visit his far-flung fleet by car. What an ignominious start.

It was a dreary period. I knew the duties of a flunkey by now but there were several differences to the shore life. There was none of the socialising with local bigwigs and much more ship visiting and entertaining ships' captains and officers. I organised the programme of visits to ships and tried to keep the Admiral informed of what was going on. The latter was a tricky matter. One had to use one's discretion as to how much to pass on from one's own social contacts and knowledge of the ships. Some captains thought the flag lieutenant was a sort of spy and if they thought I was reporting back to the Admiral I would lose their cooperation. I normally restricted myself to good news.

We were lucky in *Duke of York* in having a pleasant and intelligent 'cuddy' (naval slang for the admiral's mess), where the Admiral, his chief of staff, the captain of the fleet (head of administration), the captain of the flagship, the Admiral's secretary and I fed. The captain of the flagship was an old friend and my former captain in HMS *Mendip* during the war. We all fed at the Admiral's expense, for which he had some sort of allowance. Many decisions were taken round the table and there wasn't much social chitchat. The Admiral was a workaholic who preferred to talk 'shop', which was never dull, although I would have preferred a more gossipy conversation like my former boss used to indulge in. This admiral was quick off the mark to meals and the pre-dinner drinks session was severely rationed. You were lucky if you got more than one drink.

We travelled all over the country visiting the ships of the fleet. The drill was always the same. Arrive at the ship, the car flying the Admiral's flag on the bonnet (a red St George's Cross on a white background, such as you now see at football matches). The Admiral is 'piped' on board, meets the captain, *Rule Britannia* if they have a band, inspects the guard of honour and then meets the heads of departments. Then he walks round the ship and inspects the armament and the living quarters and anything else he particularly wants to see. After that he goes down to the captain's cabin for a chat and a restorative drink and soon we are on the way to the next victim. It gave the Admiral a fleeting impression of the ship's standard and was sometimes most revealing. By the time you became an admiral you developed a sixth sense when you visited a ship. Years later, when I was commanding a squadron of ships, I could often tell from the way the officers and men stood on parade and how they moved and answered my questions whether it was a smart outfit or not. The Admiral would sometimes turn to me after we had left and say, 'What did you think of her?' This was when I had to combine truth and tact.

Throughout the winter of 1948, this was the pattern as the fleet mouldered in harbour, while the government nationalised everything they could lay their hands on.

In May, the fuel crisis was over and the Home Fleet was sailed to Torbay to help police and organise the sailing races and maritime events for the 1948 Olympics. Torbay was a magnificent setting for the hundreds of craft racing round the great bay. It also kept me busy as the Admiral had to entertain Olympic and local personalities, some of whom didn't realise that Navy gin was much stronger than pub gin and found getting down the gangway into the barge after the party somewhat puzzling.

24

SEAGOING FLUNKEY

The 1948 Olympics were a modest affair compared with the modern events but it was a magnificent sight to see Torbay crowded with a forest of sails and watch the boats tossing and straining as they raced for Gold. At last, it did feel as if the war was over.

As soon as the Olympics were over the Admiral, unexpectedly, told his personal staff that they could take a long weekend. This was most unusual. Some of my family were at home at Belstone and I decided to surprise them. After watching the heroic efforts of the sailors in their Olympian struggles, I felt something unusual was called for so I decided to walk home from Torquay across Dartmoor, stretching the legs and eschewing all public transport.

Belstone was about 40 miles by road, including 25 miles through the wilds of the moor, but a mile on that terrain is far more testing than on footpaths. One look at the map told me I could not do it in daylight hours so I caught an early morning bus from Torquay to South Brent on the southern tip of Dartmoor, which meant I only had 25 miles to walk to reach home at the far northern extremity of the moor. Twenty-five miles does not sound a great distance but crossing Dartmoor is a hard slog, climbing up tors, crossing rivers and avoiding bogs and marshes. The first part of the walk was delightful all the way up the river Avon to its source in a wild upland marsh and on to the hamlet of Two Bridges. This was the halfway mark and a good spot for lunch at the Two Bridges Hotel. Steak and kidney pie followed by treacle tart and clotted cream. Or so I imagined. Utter disaster: the hotel was closed. I was ravenous after a 7.00 am start.

What to do? Pack it in and thumb a lift to Moreton Hampstead, 12 miles away, and then hope for a bus home. There were very few cars on the road in 1948. So on and on it was to be. We must never surrender! After all, we had just won the war, and what was another 13 miles on an empty stomach? Think of Nelson and the great deeds of the past. Press on. Unfortunately, my stomach did not seem impressed by such waffle.

Up the river Dart I staggered. My steps became weaker as I climbed to the upper reaches of the river in the remotest part of the high moor, country that I love, but not on this day. Then I remembered there was a chocolate bar in my raincoat pocket. That would keep me going. I wolfed it down and was promptly very sick, again and again.

I lay on the hillside in the heather and despaired. I was totally out of training for hillwalking and should never have attempted it. No one on board knew what I had intended to do and I had not even told my family I was coming. I imagined the headlines in the *Western Morning News*:

ADMIRAL'S AIDE DESERTS
Mystery of flag lieutenant's disappearance

Then, a few months later:

SKELETON OF UNKNOWN MALE FOUND ON DARTMOOR

All my walking experience told me I MUST keep going. To encourage myself I tried singing and, to the tune of *Onward Christian Soldiers*, I marched up the last high hill, appropriately named Hangingstone Hill and the third highest on Dartmoor. From there I could almost see home some 5 miles further on. It was downhill all the way now, following the river Taw. I reached home as daylight faded, and so did I. My family greeted me with derision.

'How stupid can you be? You must be mad; one of these days you'll kill yourself.'

Over sixty years later, I'm still going strong.

When I got back on board I kept my lips tightly buttoned and revealed nothing about my misadventure.

To shake off the sloth of the previous few months marooned in harbour, after the Olympics the Admiral and his staff had planned an intensive sea training programme in the Atlantic. After working hard all the way across the Atlantic the fleet was to enjoy a fun cruise in the Caribbean. The Admiral had fond memories of a similar cruise he had enjoyed before the war. We suspected he might have been stricken by some fair damsel in the West Indies. After all, Nelson had married a woman from the island of Nevis, Florence Nisbet, whom he later ditched in favour of his mistress, Emma Hamilton, when he was stationed in the Caribbean.

Day and night, we exercised and trained and tested the fleet's defences and attacked imaginary foes. In the brief interludes in the dog watches (from 1600-1800 and 1800-2000 hours) between exercises we enjoyed two recreations: swimming over the ship's side in mid Atlantic and deck hockey. There is a special frisson when you jump off the ship's side into the mighty ocean with over 10,000 feet of water before you could touch bottom. The whole fleet would stop engines, the signal 'Hands to Bathe' was hoisted at the yardarm and hundreds of sailors would dive off their ships into the Atlantic. Lifeboats were available.

Deck hockey is a game for lunatics, usually six a side. There are virtually no rules except that you mustn't physically attack your opponents with your stick. The goals are marked with a couple of sweaters and the ball is a wooden 'puck' (a square of wood about 4 inches across). The puck never goes out of play unless it goes over the ship's side. It's a fast and furious sport as you career round deck fittings such as ventilation 'mushrooms' and hatchways. Anyone can make up a team and challenge any other team.

We had on board as passengers Lord Hall, First Lord of the Admiralty, our top political boss, who had been a Labour MP for a Welsh constituency, and Sir John Laing, the head of the Admiralty Civil Service, the successor to Samuel Pepys, the famous diarist and seventeenth-century Secretary of the Admiralty. Part of my job was to see that our visitors were shown whatever they wanted to see and were properly cosseted and their every whim satisfied.

We fired the guns, unleashed torpedoes, flew off fighters to defend the fleet against air attack. There were night actions, dawn attacks by destroyers and air attacks at any time of the day. We were making up for the time lost when we had been beached.

To the Navy of the twenty-first century, our weapons would seem antediluvian. Our guns had a maximum range of 20 miles compared to modern missiles with ranges of more than 200 miles. The underwater range of our anti-submarine detection gear was measured in hundreds of yards whereas today it is measured in miles. Compared to modern times, the Navy of 1947 was as antique as the sailing ship navy was to the steam-engined fleet.

During the Atlantic exercises I spent as much time as possible on the Admiral's bridge, attentive to his bidding and observing the Fleet Signal Officer, whose deputy I was, but I had no hands-on responsibility for fleet communications. There was nothing that I actually had to do. I sometimes wished the Fleet Signal Officer might be stricken by some undiagnosed ailment and be carted off to hospital so that I could step into his shoes, but he remained remarkably healthy. He was both an excellent signal officer and delightful.

After ten exhausting days at sea, the fleet was split up and each ship was detached to visit different Caribbean islands. Our first port of call was Bridgetown, Barbados. It was a paradise after the drabness of post-war Britain. Barbados was then a British colony, a peaceful land of sugar canes and golden beaches, unspoiled by tourism. It was hot but not too hot and we were right royally entertained by the mainly white population, although the political power was beginning to be taken over by the larger black population. The Admiral's dinner parties on board were always carefully mixed, black and white.

On our first night in harbour the Bridgetown yacht club threw a grand ball for the officers of the fleet such as I had never seen since the hunt balls of before the war (not that I had ever been invited to one). Many of our hosts and all the glitterati of Barbados had been invited by the Admiral (guest list provided by the Governor) to a cocktail party on the quarterdeck of the flagship. This was quite an occasion with the band playing popular tunes, coloured lights strung all around the quarterdeck awning and officers dressed up in their best dinner uniform. As soon as the party was over the Admiral told me he could do without me for the rest of the evening and I could go to the ball, rather like Cinderella. I went ashore with a group of friends, intent on having a huge whale of a time.

The yacht club was on some sort of a pier or pontoon jutting out over the water and it had been enclosed in a marquee. The setting for the ball was magical, with a dance floor over the sea and a multicoloured awning above also festooned with fairy lights that reflected in the waters of the bay. It was truly romantic.

The young ladies of the island wore long ball gowns and the men were in white tuxedoes with black cummerbunds and black bow ties. We weren't outsmarted with our naval uniform, mess undress (nothing undressed about it), a short jacket buttoned across the waist with gilt buttons and the gold lace of our rank on the sleeves, bow tie and miniature medals, if we had any, on the lapel. Naval uniform was usually guaranteed to attract the ladies, which we hoped it would that evening.

In the midst of this fairyland I saw a vision, a damsel in a long white ball dress of such beauty that she took my breath away. I was stricken as if by a bolt of lightning and fell instantly in love. A *coup de foudre*, I think the French call it. This does sometimes happen when you have been at sea a long time.

But I was sitting at the wrong table. How could I reach a position of encounter from where I could strike? With the help of my friends we edged close to her table and barged in on her party, who seemed quite pleased to meet some sailor boys. Now, how to show her how special (peculiar?) I was? On the table there was a vase of daffodils and I plucked a bloom and ate it, explaining that I always ate daffodils as a salad before the main course. It had the desired effect. Oddball or lunatic, but intriguing, she told me later. We danced. We danced all night. For the rest of our visit, whenever I was allowed out, we swam and danced at the local beach club near her home, and the sea was particularly blue and the moon twice as bright.

I was restricted in my shore going because the Admiral's official duties called me to his side. After the ball I had to be up again at 0700 hours to prepare for a day of official calls and sightseeing with my boss. On our second evening the Admiral held a big dinner party for all the local top officials from the Governor downwards. My job was to meet the guests on the jetty and escort them on board in the Commander-in-Chief's barge. On the way back to the ship I had to memorise their names so that I could introduce them personally to the Admiral. I always assumed that the lady of a couple was a Mrs of the same name and trusted that the man hadn't brought his mistress.

ABANDON SHIP!

The Admiral was an excellent host and after dinner he would lead us up on deck and we'd saunter around the quarterdeck in the evening breeze, sipping brandy and liqueurs. At midnight the barge would waft them all ashore.

The Admiral was remarkably tolerant and when he had a dinner party ashore he would say, 'I think I can manage without you tonight, Tony.' So once I had seen him into the barge I would rush ashore myself and meet my girlfriend and friends who had gone ashore earlier at the beach club. The club had a good calypso band, excellent West Indian food and the powerful white rum. We'd dance the night away and swim when it got too hot. We'd crawl back on board about 2.00 am. I had to be up and about and reasonably perky by 7.30 am. If I was noticeably hung-over the Admiral never commented on it and we fulfilled a packed programme of official engagements each day.

Before we left I was bidden to tea by my girlfriend's mother and father in their grand bungalow above an Atlantic bay. After bathing and tea I was plied with Planter's Punch, a delicious cool drink that tasted like an exotic fruit juice. It was made with white rum and the juice of fresh limes and it was a very deceptive cocktail. To the novice it didn't seem to have any punch at all. How wrong could you be? It slowly dawned on me that I had no legs. Luckily, I was sitting down. I felt perfectly sober and my brain was working normally but below the hips nothing, no feeling. I thought I should remain seated and switch to long, soft drinks in the hope that I would recover before we had to go out to dinner.

Somehow, the conversation got round to how the drink was made and my host warned me (too late) that it was much stronger than it appeared. By this time I was only half legless. I owned up and we had a good laugh and eventually a swim to complete the recovery.

All too soon the magical days came to an end as our stay drew to a finale. Then it was one last, wonderful evening at the beach club making merry and long and painful farewells before catching the last liberty boat back to the ship.

After the social explosion that had been Barbados, the Admiral felt the fleet needed hard work and sobriety and the Home Fleet rendezvoused at the then remote island of Tobago, well away from the fleshpots. There we engaged in what was called General Drill, which was a series of competitive seamanship exercises for ships in harbour.

'All ships let go second anchor and weigh anchor by hand.'

'Mount machine gun in picket boats.'

'Signal to the flagship by semaphore the height of the highest mountain in Antarctica.'

'Midshipmen lower lifeboat and row round the ship.'

And so on, part serious and part amusement. By the end of General Drill crews were exhausted and ships were left with equipment strewn over the deck.

Having restored our health the fleet split up again to enjoy another series of 'show the flag' visits. Our slot was Antigua. The Governor, His Excellency Oliver Baldwin, was the son of Stanley Baldwin, who had been the prime minister of Great Britain that had engineered the abdication of King Edward VIII in 1936. The gossip wheel told us that he had been sent to the West Indies to get him out of the limelight as he was an enthusiastic homosexual, which at that time was a criminal matter. The word 'gay' was not then used and simply meant a jolly, lively and amusing person. Our island liaison official confirmed the gossip when he warned us, with a wink, that the young midshipmen should keep their 'backs to the wall' when talking to His Excellency as he had a proclivity for young gentlemen. Not very useful advice. The Governor threw a dinner party for the Admiral and his staff and I did notice there were several 'pretty boys' amongst the waiters. As far as I know, none of our young men were propositioned.

After the enticements of Antigua our last Caribbean call was Kingston, the capital of Jamaica, home of the Calypso bands. *Brown Skin Girl* was then number one in the charts. There they had a different problem. The men were not fussy about getting married and they were highly promiscuous and preferred mobile relationships. So Molly Huggins, the Governor's wife, a feisty blonde, had decided to try and encourage the Jamaicans to take up matrimony. She spent large sums (her own or social services'?) buying cheap wedding rings, which she handed out to couples in the hope that it would encourage them to live a more settled life and stay faithful. It didn't work.

ABANDON SHIP!

Our visit to Kingston was purely social, showing the flag and waving it for the Empire. On arrival the usual list of hosts who were offering to entertain officers and sailors went up on the notice boards and by now we were experts at spotting the winners. 'Two daughters, a swimming pool and a private beach' – a high score, but I and two friends were after something out of the ordinary and we plumped for a farm in the hills outside Kingston, to see something of the countryside. The Admiral had a private engagement so I was let off the leash.

Locals who offered their hospitality were known to us as 'barons' as they were usually wealthy and had opulent establishments. A large car came to pick us up and we drove out to an impressive mansion set in the hills above Kingston with rolling farmland all around. They were obviously 'horsey' people as there was a large stable yard and lots of horses' heads sticking out of their boxes. I didn't know one end of a horse from the other and wondered if I had made a wrong choice of host. When we sat down for lunch I found myself sitting next to my host's wife.

'Whereabouts do you live in England?' she enquired.

'On Dartmoor, in Devon,' I replied.

This is where I made a terrible mistake. Thinking to get on a wavelength with her, I added, 'There is a special breed of pony on the moor known as Dartmoor ponies,' and I proceeded to give her a potted history of the Dartmoors: originally pit ponies down the mines, then pet food when the mines packed up and perhaps steaks in France.

'Can you ride them?' she asked.

'Well, I have ridden them,' I said. But I forgot to say it had been about fifteen years ago and I had never mounted a horse since. Sometimes when we are a little unsure of ourselves in an unfamiliar social milieu we pretend to rather more knowledge than we really have.

Out to lunch and there is a tennis court: 'Do you play tennis?' asks your hostess.

'Er, I have.' But you forget to say you haven't played since you left school. Before you know where you are you are on the court in a mixed doubles with a fierce female partner who won the tennis club doubles last year.

SEAGOING FLUNKEY

So when I said I had ridden Dartmoor ponies, I may have given the impression that I had roamed far and wide over the hills and valleys of the moor.

'You must try one of our stallions,' she said.

What had I let myself in for? Still, after a couple of rum cocktails I felt up for anything. Actually, my riding career had been brief. Fifteen years earlier, when I was fourteen, my mother decided the whole family should learn to ride. We were on holiday on Dartmoor at Lydford, near Tavistock. Introduced to a horsey lady with iron-cropped hair and a moustache she told us: 'No need for saddles and stirrups today, just a gentle run-in; grip hard with your thighs and hold the reins well up.' There were a few more tips on horse control and we were off. I looked at my steed and could see he didn't much care for T.McC and the feeling was reciprocated. I clambered onto his back and that was the signal for him to set off at speed. I lost the reins and only stayed on by clutching him round his neck until he suddenly stopped and I went straight over his head into a clump of heather. Not a great start. The next day I tried again and ended up embracing the heather for a second time. Pony and I never got on friendly terms and I had never ridden since.

I now realised I had made the most colossal boob and hoped that by the end of a sumptuous lunch my hostess would forget her invitation.

It had always been drummed into us as young officers that when we were ashore we must remember we were ambassadors for England and the Empire. Always be prepared for any venture (the Scout motto); show what you are made of.

Thus I was led to the slaughter. A massive beast was led out of his stable. One of my friends was already mounted but he was a horseman. The third member of our party had sensibly declined all knowledge of equine matters and was quietly smirking in the background.

I somehow climbed up onto the horse's massive frame and actually sat in the saddle holding the reins. Perhaps it wasn't so difficult, after all. We moved smoothly out of the stable yard. OK so far. It was actually quite enjoyable (we'd had an excellent lunch). My friend trotted off and this seemed to give my steed the idea to have a bit of fun and he suddenly took off like a force ten hurricane. Like fifteen years earlier, I lost all control and ended up horizontal with my arms tight around the horse's neck, reins loose and stirrups dangling. My only aim now was to stay on the blighter. Then, thankfully, before I fell off he lost interest and ambled back. He knew his rider was useless. Somehow I got myself back into the saddle with the reins in my hands and rode in stately fashion back to the house. I have never made the same mistake again.

'Do you ride?'

'Definitely not.'

After the Caribbean visits we sailed up the east coast of America to Norfolk, Virginia, to visit the American Atlantic Fleet and pay an official call on the United States Navy Chief of Operations in Washington. We then sailed on to Bermuda on the way home. Bermuda had been colonised by English settlers in 1612 and was currently the headquarters of the British West Indies Naval Squadron. With the rundown of the Navy it would soon be closed and taken over by the Americans.

There was the usual round of the private and official cocktail parties, dinner parties and a range of sporting events. These were beginning to pall after our marathon of parties throughout our visits to so many Caribbean islands. But the cruise had been a wonderful experience of pre-war opulence and colour and the bubbles of life that we had forgotten in the long years of austerity. It had been exhilarating to mingle with people who had escaped the stresses and dangers of a long war and to enjoy fleeting romances with beautiful women.

Arriving in Portsmouth, England, life seemed a little dull after the romance and excitement of the New World. I enjoyed Christmas leave at home on Dartmoor, where the family gathered, and despite the still heavy food rationing we got the Christmas spirit and amused ourselves. Three years after the war, bread and sweets were still rationed as well as meat, eggs, butter and most other foodstuffs.

In May 1948, I had been promoted to Lieutenant Commander, an automatic promotion and not dependent on merit or good behaviour. In January, the fleet enjoyed its traditional spring cruise, avoiding the harsh English winter. The excuse was to exercise with the Med Fleet, then as powerful as the Home Fleet. Both fleets foregathered in Gibraltar Harbour, which was stuffed with ships of the combined fleets, and when we went to sea we fought inter-fleet battles to hone our fighting skills. While in harbour the two fleets fought spirited battles on the sports fields with great ferocity. Old Dartmouth friends were reunited in the evenings in the bars of the narrow main street.

At the end of our exercises at the end of March, by which time the warmth of spring might have come to Britain, the Home Fleet departed for home and the Med Fleet returned to Malta. On the way home we called in at Lisbon to represent our country on the occasion of the 500th anniversary of the signing of the Anglo-Portuguese Treaty of 1449. This is our oldest treaty but none of us had heard of it and we had quickly to revise our history.

It was a purely social occasion and we represented the King and Britain with aplomb at many cocktail and dinner parties. One particular lunch party, which sticks in my mind, was the Portuguese Government's official lunch to commemorate the anniversary, with tables festooned with miniature Portuguese and British flags and serried rows of senior and elderly Portuguese naval and military officers and as many of our top brass as we could muster, plus me.

Why was I there? Not for any special attributes but simply because I was attached to my admiral. We were in one of the royal palaces, no longer royal as they had kicked out their king years earlier and it was now used for government entertaining.

I found myself plonked down between two senior and ancient Portuguese naval officers who had not a word of English, and I knew even less Portuguese. Each of the twelve courses was complemented by a different wine in very small glasses. As the wine opened up my spirits I did my best to engage the two ancients on either side of me in dialogue by hand signals and smiles, indicating what a lovely day it was and how much I was enjoying the delicious food, what a wonderful place and so on, but it didn't seem to add to the gaiety of the nations and I wondered if they thought I was a bit uppity. After the fourth course I relapsed into silence and dreamed of my forthcoming leave on Dartmoor.

Lunch started at 2.00 pm and after the twelfth course and the speeches we got away at 5.00 pm. Then it was back to HMS *Duke of York* for some rest before the next evening engagement, having first ensured that the Admiral was also flat on his back and needing no service from me. In my deepest sleep there came a rat-a-tat-tat on my door and a somewhat flustered Portuguese naval liaison officer appeared. Luckily, he spoke some English.

'The Portuguese Government wishes to present a most prestigious medal to your admiral, the Order of Jesu Christo (First Class). Please tell me what is the correct procedure.'

I remembered my briefing notes on 'Our Visit to Our Oldest Ally': 'All proposed medals and decorations must receive the prior approval of His Majesty's Government.' Rather pompously, I informed the good commander of this edict, but added, 'Your admiral could make a direct enquiry of my admiral.'

He didn't think so. Then he added, possibly as an inducement, 'If your admiral receives the Order of Jesu Christo you too will be receiving the Order of Jesu Christo (4th Class). It is a very beautiful medallion.'

What a temptation. I wondered if he was after an MBE. However, I reiterated, 'All decorations, even to the lower orders like myself, have to be approved by the British Government.'

Crestfallen, he departed to consult his masters. We heard no more and there was no follow-up to the British Admiralty. Had he been carried away by the excellent lunch? It was one of those bizarre little episodes that naval service presents. Never a dull moment.

After Lisbon we sailed for the UK and more war exercises. We were 'attacked' by the RAF and by our own submarines throughout the twenty-four hours as we approached the Bay of Biscay and the Channel. By the time we reached Portsmouth we were ready for our Easter leave.

After Easter leave the Admiral transferred his flag from the battleship *Duke of York* to the aircraft carrier *Implacable*. He believed the day of the big battleship was over and that the Fleet Air Arm was the fleet's main attack weapon and he wanted to reinforce this stance by flying his flag in a carrier. I'm sure he was right; many junior officers had been saying that even before the Second World War.

The fleet 'worked up' at Portland and then split to make foreign and home visits to show the flag. Our visits were well chosen by the Admiral's staff and we took off for the Baltic to call on the Norwegians and the Danes. We sailed first to Oslo, where we were given a tremendous welcome. At that time Norway had a special affection for the British Navy as it had rescued their king and his family in 1940, when the Germans had invaded Norway. We had also landed the liberating troops in 1945. Throughout the war many Norwegians had made the hazardous journey in fishing boats across the North Sea to the Shetland Islands, their escape allowing them then to fight the enemy. Like the Vikings before them, many of them had carried off Scottish girls into marriage.

King Haakon was an honorary British admiral and he came onboard with Crown Prince Olav to inspect the ship's company. On the first evening the Admiral threw a grand dinner party for the Norwegian royals and government ministers. The King, who was a widower, looked like a happy heron – long, gangly and smiling. He was a jolly and informal man and put us at our ease. All the family spoke impeccable English. It was one of our best dinner parties.

The following afternoon, *Implacable* threw a children's party, mainly for the war orphans of Oslo. The flight deck and aircraft hangar below were transformed into a cross between a funfair and fairyland, with all sorts of sideshows from pirates' caves, fortune tellers and treasure grottoes to water chutes, slides and roundabouts. Being natural child entertainers, the sailors revelled in dressing up in hilarious costumes such as wild animals, pirates and grotesques of every description. I was deputed to make sure the royal grandchildren enjoyed themselves, amongst whom was the future heir to the throne, Prince Harald, then a lively boy of ten or eleven. My task was easy as they were great fun and joined in with the other children and had a splendid time, even insisting I take them down the steep slide on my back. Not good for my best uniform.

I doubt if it is realised at home what credit these flag-showing visits achieved for Britain. We hosted special visits for war disabled and various specialist groups and the ship was open to the public each afternoon, when they could troop on board and poke around. Ashore our sports teams played every sport against local teams and were entertained by the local clubs. In representing their nation this way, the crew must have interacted with thousands of Norwegians.

The next stop was Copenhagen, which had also been liberated by the British four years earlier. I had fond memories of Copenhagen from 1936, when my first ship, the training cruiser HMS *Frobisher*, tied up alongside the Langelinie Jetty near the statue of the Little Mermaid. We young sailors had dated some of the blonde beauties strolling up and down the jetty who were seemingly hoping for an encounter. Also on this stop, the King had invited twenty *Frobisher* cadets to lunch at his summer palace at Amelienborg, which was a huge pleasure that included vintage champagne and young Copenhagen beauties walking with us around the garden.

Danish visits were indeed real fun trips, but my recollections of the 1949 one are now hazy. Had the festivities of Oslo been too much for me? The Admiral had certainly entertained the Danish Royals but I must have become rather blasé about meeting kings and princesses because I don't recall being involved.

After all this frivolity the summer cruise ended in a hurricane of international exercises in the Western Approaches. By mid-1949, the Cold War was hotting up. As the forerunner to the North Atlantic Treaty Organisation (NATO), a force known as the Western European Union (WEU) had been established. This consisted of French, Dutch, Belgian, Norwegian, Danish and British forces, with Field Marshal Montgomery of Alamein as Supreme Commander. For our first naval exercises WEU navies assembled in Mount's Bay in Cornwall. Our admiral was in overall charge of the naval manoeuvres, but it was mostly a social occasion and I remember the dinner parties we gave rather than the very elementary sea exercises. We were a new outfit, feeling our way.

The WEU didn't last long as it was subsumed into NATO later in 1949. By this time, the wartime alliance with the Russians had fragmented and the countries that the Soviets had occupied at the end of the Second World War became dominated by the USSR and were ruthlessly ruled by local communist bosses. Europe had once again dissolved into two opposing blocs. The USSR dominated East Germany, Bulgaria, Romania, Hungary, Poland, Czechoslovakia, Yugoslavia, the Baltic States and parts of Austria, and NATO supported the western states of Europe.

The important distinction of the post-Second World War situation was that the Americans remained in Europe instead of retreating into isolationism as they had after the First World War. This was due to the farsightedness of President Harry Truman who, on 12 March 1947, had set out his policy of 'Containment', which became known as the Truman Doctrine. This stated that:

> It must be the policy of the United States of America to help free peoples who are resisting subjugation by armed minorities or outside pressure.

Its purpose was to contain the Soviet Union and prevent it expanding its influence into other countries such as Greece. This marked the acceptance by the US of the leadership of the free world and meant that American forces would remain in Europe as a shield against further communist aggression.

In the same year, General George Marshal, the American Secretary of State, in a speech at Harvard University, had set out his European Recovery Programme, entirely financed by the US. Over the next four years, $13 billion was poured into the free countries of Western Europe. The UK received twenty-five per cent of the total. This was the impetus that regenerated Western European economies after the devastation of the war years and must have been one of the most generous acts ever. The final brick in the post-war structure was the signing of the North Atlantic Treaty on 4 April 1949 (forming the basis for NATO), designed to contain the USSR, consisting of the US and Canada and the free nations of Western Europe.

To my generation it seemed incredible that we were once again facing the possibility of war. We had been born under the shadow of the First World War and were reared in the uneasy inter-war years, when the peoples of Europe prayed that there would never be a return to the terrible slaughter of the Western Front offensives in France. Yet war had broken out again in September 1939, after Germany invaded Poland, and my generation had become the fodder for six more long years of war.

The overall death toll of the Second World War dwarfed that of the 1914-1918 figures. First World War military deaths are recorded as 8,542,015. The civilian death toll was not recorded, but was relatively small. In the Second World War, the total number of military deaths was in the region of 14,662,000, but the truly ghastly figure was the number of civilians killed – around 27,000,000. Of these, between sixteen and seventeen million were Russian civilians slaughtered by the advancing German Army. On top of this, the Holocaust obliterated another six to seven million Jews, making an incredible total of nearly fifty million dead. Yes, Europe had gone mad.

With the return to peace in 1945, I hoped we had seen the end of war. Yet here we were, only four years on, teetering on the brink of a far more terrible prospect – nuclear war and the possibility of world annihilation.

The consequences of another world war were so horrendous that I shut my mind to it. I had none of the dilemmas that had affected me in the run-up to the Second World War, when my anti-war feelings had changed to wholehearted acceptance of the need to fight. This time, with the potential enormity of the situation, I felt insignificant, and that any contribution I made would have negligible effect.

I did not actually believe that the Russians would attack the West in an all-out war. At that time they had no nuclear weapons, whereas the Americans did. The Soviets were far more likely to nibble away at the edges of Europe when one of the local communist parties looked as if it had the capacity to topple a government, as they nearly did in the Greek Civil War of 1946-1949. I was more concerned that the Americans, with their nuclear arsenal, might inadvertently react to a false alarm, particularly a few years later, when the Russians had developed their own nuclear capability. So, for the third time in the calamitous twentieth century, we faced possible death and destruction.

SEAGOING FLUNKEY

Looking back at those times, the formation of NATO succeeded in halting communist aggression and may well have prevented another war.

After the Western Union exercises the fleet dispersed to its home ports of Portsmouth, Plymouth and Chatham for the summer break. Throughout the summer I had been suffering intermittent stomach pains, which the doctor put down to the stresses of the job. I didn't really agree with him but I never argued with doctors. They might have one under the knife sometime and it was best to keep on the right side of them. The offending appendix was removed in the naval hospital at Plymouth.

Once recovered, I rejoined my admiral in time for the autumn cruise. Being a Scot, he decided to take the fleet to the north. This was usual at this time of year when the fleet traditionally sailed to Invergordon in the Moray Firth for an intensive period of weapons training and seamanship exercises, well away from the fleshpots of the soft south.

It was not all hair shirt and hard living because it was also the season of the Highland balls, and the officers of the fleet were expected to provide a male stimulus to these upper-crust events. A typical ball started after a dinner party at 10.00 pm and went on through the night until breakfast at 6.00 am. Throughout the night there were two bands performing, one playing exclusively Scottish reels, while the other jazzed away to the music of the era in a separate ballroom. In Inverness the Scots took their Scottish dancing very seriously and the Admiral was an expert, so I felt compelled to display my limited skills. With the help of malt whisky I made up for any lack of skill with vigour and panache. Arriving back on board at 7.00 am, we had the usual Sunday routine of church to get through.

Scotland in late autumn is at its most beautiful and there was time at weekends for sailing and picnics in the long evenings when we were in harbour. By the beginning of December we were on our way back to Portsmouth and we called in to the Firth of Clyde to show the flag to Glaswegians and the towns on the Firth. There we gave a lunch for the Lord Provost of Glasgow and the mayors of Greenock and other

41

Firth towns. I did not remind the Mayor of Greenock of a wartime escapade on the local golf course when a posse of us landed from our ship and played cowboys and Indians on the hills above the local golf course and strayed onto the fairway to the fury of the players. Happy days of foolish youth.

My time in the Home Fleet was coming to an end as the Admiral was hauling down his flag and my flag lieutenancy was nearly over, and none too soon. It had been a fascinating time but socially gruelling. The Admiral couldn't have been nicer but he wasn't one for letting his hair down, although he allowed me to let mine down occasionally. For three years in the Home Fleet and at Plymouth I had tried to overcome my natural disinclination for the flunkey's job and I seemed to have convinced my two admirals that I was reasonably OK as they both gave me glowing testimonials.

When I looked back at my life amongst the top brass I appreciated the opportunities I'd had to have been in contact with many of the brightest and best, with many future admirals amongst the ships' commanding officers. This would stand me in good stead in promotion steeplechases. It's who you know, not what you know, what counts.

Chapter 5

Teacher

I had a new appointment to take up in January as an instructor at the main naval Signal School at Leydene House, near Petersfield, in Hampshire. The last time I had visited the house, now HMS *Mercury*, had been in the middle of the war, in 1942, as an unwilling conscript student to become a specialist signal officer. Then, I had felt guilty at being ashore in the middle of a desperate war. Now, I was delighted, as teaching was a role I much enjoyed. The job was to train young officers to become specialist signal officers, a sort of post-graduate course for bright young men in from the sea, and extremely challenging to one who was only about five years older than they were. I was looking forward to it.

The school's main building was an Edwardian mansion standing on a ridge of the South Downs above the river Meon. If you chose the right place to sit at meals you could, on a fine day, see the Solent dancing with reflected sunlight, and the Isle of Wight beyond. Two miles to the west along the ridge lay Winchester Hill, the site of a Roman fort, and one mile to the east was Butser Hill, the highest point on the South Downs. Portsmouth lay 16 miles to the south, hidden behind Portsdown Hill.

The grandeur of the mansion had been spoilt by a number of temporary buildings that had spawned all around its parkland to provide classrooms and accommodation quarters. From the terraces of the main house the park fell away down the hillside and merged into beautiful beech woods that hid any sign of civilisation.

The Navy had requisitioned the house and its grounds in 1940, when the old Signal School in Portsmouth was bombed out. The house belonged to the Peel family, not ancient lineage aristocrats, but new money, the legacy of a successful linoleum millionaire. Quite naturally, Lady Peel was not keen about being kicked out of her home, but there was no argument in wartime. The Navy needed it and the Navy got it. I believe she had other residences. The story handed down was that, when the Captain of the Signal School called on Lady Peel to explain the necessity of the requisition, the butler introduced him as, 'The man from the dockyard to see you madam. Shall I show him in?'

The daily life we led in the 1950s seems prehistoric by today's standards. The day began with a wake-up call from one's young Wren steward and a pot of tea. Breakfast followed at 8.00 am, porridge or cereal, followed by fish or eggs, or both if you were hungry. Of course, then there was toast and marmalade and tea or coffee. Then you were ready for the rigours of the day. Mid-morning there was a short coffee break to keep you going till lunchtime, which was always three courses – soup, a meat joint or fish, pudding, cheese and biscuits, followed by coffee. That was enough to put most students to sleep in the afternoon session and I used to have to resort to violent tactics to keep them awake.

The classroom day finished between 4.00 pm and 4.30 pm with afternoon tea and cake. After that it was time to prepare the next day's lectures and then play squash, tennis or go for a walk. Exercise was essential to prepare for the main meal of the day – a formal dinner. You could skip dinner and have a light buffet supper of only two courses, but you were expected to attend dinner frequently. That meant dressing up in evening dress uniform, and pre-dinner drinks at the bar to stiffen one up for the four-course meal to follow, which consisted of soup, main course (always meat; no specials for 'veggies'), sweets and a savoury such as devils or angels on horseback, or mushrooms on toast. Then the tables were cleared, except for bowls of fruit, for the ceremony of 'Passing the Port' and the loyal toast. Port decanters were placed in front of the President (the Commander) and at the opposite end of the table, Mr Vice, the next most senior officer. Decanters were then carefully rotated in a clockwise direction down both sides of the table. There was to be NO DRINKING BEFORE THE LOYAL

TEACHER

TOAST – a trap that civilian guests sometimes fell into. Your guest was your responsibility and should you allow him to commit such a grievous crime, you paid for it according to some punishment meted out by the president.

'Mr (always Mr, until one became a commander) McCrum will pay for a glass of port for his two next-door neighbours.' This added two shillings to my wine bill.

Then the president called out, 'Mr Vice, the King.'

He responded with, 'Ladies and Gentlemen, the King,' because by this time, ladies were part of the Navy.

There was a tendency for guests to try and stand up for the loyal toast but naval officers had always remained seated since King William IV had risen for the loyal toast and hit his head on the deckhead. Thenceforth, he declared, officers should remain seated during the loyal toast. The more sceptical and irreverent officers believed it was more likely that many of the officers, including the King, had imbibed liberally and were unable to stand.

Then came the farewell speeches, if there were any leavers, and after those, we transferred to the ante room for liqueurs or brandy, Cointreau, Benedictine, Grand Marnier and many others. It's a wonder any of us reached seventy.

We did also work quite hard: parade every day at 8.45 am to salute the White Ensign being hoisted at the masthead, and at 9.00 am, the first classroom session. There was a short break at 10.15 am and another session from 10.30-12.00. In the afternoons there were classroom periods until 4.00 pm and the students were expected to revise on their own in the evenings, as did I, to try and keep one chapter ahead of my class, which included some exceedingly clever young officers who enjoyed trying to trip me up. It was a pleasure to teach such interesting and able young officers, who had just come in from sea and were full of *joie de vivre*.

In June 1951, I was taken by surprise when my name came up in the promotion stakes for the rank of commander. Promotion to commander is the first occasion when promotion in the Navy is selective. Up to this rank my promotions had been automatic, depending on time served. Twice a year, promotion lists from

45

lieutenant commander to commander and from commander to captain were teleprinted from the Admiralty at a set time and anxious candidates hung around, hoping their name would come up. It was like waiting for exam results.

Being only thirty-two, it had never occurred to me that my name might come up on the list and I was in Portsmouth when the announcement was made. When I got back at lunchtime I was surprised and appalled by the number of officers waiting to toast my promotion to commander at my expense.

My young ex-Navy brother, at that time a schoolmaster at Rugby School, arrived that afternoon for a weekend visit and I invited a few close friends to a discreet party in my cabin that evening to further celebrate my promotion. After a few extremely dry martinis we had got up steam and began dancing eightsome reels. Scottish dancing was all the rage at that time. Music was provided by the voices of those who thought they knew the tunes. My dear brother always enjoyed a party and had a head for the hard stuff like a rock of Dartmoor granite. As we circled merrily around, his partner let go of his arm and he lost his balance and tottered backwards, coming into contact with my wardrobe. This had two full-length doors, one of them faced with a long mirror. He chose to fall against the mirrored door and, being a hefty young man, all of 6 foot 2 inches, he disappeared through the door, splintering the mirror as he went and ending up immersed in my uniform suits. Miraculously, he was unharmed, protected by my scattered clothing, but I had to pay for a new cupboard. After that we all needed a final stiff martini to steady our nerves before dinner.

I was young for the rank and I suspect the promotion was due to the number of admirals and captains I had known in my three years as a flag lieutenant. Knowing the top brass had paid off and the money came in handy. The terms passed, teaching, examining and socialising. It was hard work but a lot of fun. We were in the most beautiful part of Hampshire astride the track of what is now known as the South Downs Way, and you could walk, as I did one weekend, all the way to Eastbourne along the Downs with fantastic views of the sea to the south and pastoral countryside to the north.

Life at this time had a number of surprises, the first having been the unexpected promotion. Then one day I was summoned to the Commander's office to be told that I had been selected to accompany King George VI and Queen Elizabeth on a tour of Australia and New Zealand. I was to be one of three naval officers on the tour, along with a naval doctor and a navigator. I was the senior executive officer and communications specialist, which may sound rather grand, but my main task was to ensure that the telephone service from the royal yacht to Buckingham Palace and the government was always in working order. With me would be a team of radio operators, signalmen and Post Office engineers. As there was no royal yacht in 1952, the Shaw Savill liner SS *Gothic* had been requisitioned and converted by the Admiralty.

I was told to keep this news absolutely secret until it had been announced in the media. To say I was flabbergasted by the appointment was an understatement. I had never had any connections with royalty and felt apprehensive about mixing with such exotic creatures. Would I do? It would be terrible if I was sent home in disgrace for some awful failure to observe the correct royal protocol, but there were still some weeks of the more humdrum life at the Signal School before I was let loose into this rarefied world.

I was glad of all this excitement because it was a dispiriting period in our history as well as for the Royal Navy. The Empire was vanishing and the Navy was being run down. No longer did our squadrons command the seas of the world and Britain had not really found a role in the post-war world. Britain had exhausted herself economically and physically by her all-out effort in the six years of war. This exhaustion also seemed to affect the government, and Prime Minister Attlee's second government only lasted eighteen months before he went to the country in 1951 and was booted out. Churchill, now a very old man, was returned to power. For the first time, I voted Tory, but I felt slightly ashamed.

Luckily, I was totally absorbed in my work. I discovered that I much enjoyed teaching and training the young and the time whistled past. I was still unmarried, despite the attractions of young Wren officers.

As had happened so many times before, the time had come to say goodbye to good friends, many of whom I would never see again.

Chapter 6

Royal Tour 1952

In the New Year I joined the converted royal yacht, SS *Gothic*, which was being refitted in Birkenhead, a dismal shipbuilding town on the opposite side of the river Mersey to Liverpool. Along with the ship, the crew had also been requisitioned, including a specially selected Shaw Savill senior captain. Much tact would be needed by the naval contingent, which was really an excrescence on the rest of the liner's ship's company. We provided the crew for the royal barge, the telephone service to Buckingham Palace and the worldwide radio communications to and from the ship. The doctor was on standby for any royal medical emergencies in mid-ocean. The RN navigator had a particularly tricky balancing act, ensuring the ship kept exactly to her schedule, as the Captain had his own Merchant Navy navigator.

The jewel in the naval crown was the Royal Marine band, under the direction of Vivian Dunn, the Director of Music. They could play anything from vibrant marches to dance music and jazz. Their classic show, which was performed in each harbour visited and would be at every stop on the royal tour, was the *Ceremony of Sunset*, played when the band marched up and down the jetty belting out nautical tunes. The emotional finale started with an evening hymn, usually *Abide with Me*, played to a hushed audience. This was followed by the massed buglers sounding *The Last Post* and finally, *Sunset*, which I always thought was one of the most haunting tunes. On tour, this ceremonial took place during evening cocktail parties as the sun went down, but if sunset didn't fit in with the climax of the party, it was played anyway, even if the sun was still high in the heavens.

ABANDON SHIP!

After my team and I joined the ship in Birkenhead, we sailed down to Southampton for a final sprucing up before setting forth as a royal yacht. Luckily, we three RN officers got on famously. We weren't overawed by the royal trappings of the job and we had a lot of laughs over some of the royal procedures that were explained to us by members of the royal household who were on board. The really top brass of the royal household did not come on board to begin with but were due to join the ship on arrival in Mombasa. We had the second eleven with us and they were a mixed bunch. The more senior staff was delightful but lower down in the pecking order, some were excessively conscious of their own limited importance.

On the way through the Irish Sea we heard that the King had lung cancer and would not now be making the tour. Instead, the then Princess Elizabeth and her husband, Prince Philip, would take his place. The King was comparatively young, only fifty-six. With our new passenger line-up we had much the same job to do, although we felt we had come down a peg, but it might be more fun. We sailed from Southampton on a cold January day for Mombasa in Kenya. This was to give *Gothic* and her crew and the naval teams a 'shake-down' cruise before the royal tour began. Everything had to be immaculate and the arrivals and departures at ports had to be perfectly timed. The many worldwide radio circuits had to be tuned and tested and the royal telephone checked.

On our trip round Africa we practised the formalities of ceremonial arrivals and departures at each port we visited – Sierra Leone, Cape Town and finally, Mombasa. The Royal Marine band played stirring tunes as we entered or left harbour. As the anchor went down or as the first mooring wire was passed to the jetty, a synchronised series of events took place. The royal barge was launched into the water, the gangways were lowered and the ship was 'dressed overall'. This was the trickiest part of the procedure and involved a long string of flags being hoisted on high, stretching from bow to stern, supported by the masts. It was very easy to get the flags tangled up in the rigging or the funnel or, even worse, if some matelot's leg got caught up in the supporting wires and he found himself being hoisted on high.

At each arrival the barge ferried 'King and Queen' stand-ins to simulate the royals arriving at the jetty and the boat drill was closely scrutinised. It was quite a carry-on. By the time we reached Mombasa we were word-perfect and raring to be off.

On the cruise we heard from the household staff that Princess Elizabeth and Prince Philip enjoyed playing games, particularly charades, where one team tries to guess the subject of a scene being silently acted by a member of the other team. The team with the larger number of correct guesses wins. Coming from a family of games players this gave me the opportunity to try out some that we played at home. I had to be carefully selective because some of them might not be suitable for the more refined royal entourage. I introduced a number of more decorous games that passed the censors and we played those in the evenings to relieve the tedium of the voyage.

Such diversions did not stop us preparing with great thoroughness for the arrival of the royal party and for all the contingencies that might arise on the tour. There would be a lot of entertaining on board and we would be expected to play our part as hosts. There would be none of the more raucous behaviour that we sometimes enjoyed in ships' wardrooms. Strict sobriety and welcoming smiles would be the order of the day. I did sometimes worry that I might not be able to behave to the high standards required on a royal cruise. I had always enjoyed occasions of 'letting off steam'.

By the time *Gothic* arrived in Mombasa for the start of the tour we were ready for the excitement of the arrival on board of Princess Elizabeth and Prince Philip. They were flying out to Nairobi and having a few days' holiday in one of the game parks.

Then, just two days before the royals were due to arrive on board, a calamity hit the naval team. One of the royal barge's crew, an able seaman, was stabbed by one of the Merchant Navy stewards. So the barge's crew was short of one vital member. Worse was to follow. When the Captain and I investigated the crime we unearthed a triangular web of homosexual lovers. At this time, homosexuality was still a serious crime. The able seaman was gay and he had succeeded in attracting a young merchant seaman away from his steward lover, who stabbed our man in a fit of jealousy.

The Captain and I were faced with a Royal Navy and Merchant Navy affray. He had no authority over the able seaman and I had none over the steward so we had to reach a joint solution. We didn't know whether there were any further ramifications. Was there a clutch of homosexual sailors on the ship? What were we to do? If the press got hold of the story I could see the headlines:

NEST OF QUEERS IN THE ROYAL YACHT

NAVAL MAN STABBED BY JEALOUS SAILOR

It would be a catastrophic start to Princess Elizabeth's first big independent tour. The Captain and I decided to try and keep the incident under wraps until we sailed. He dealt with the stabber and I seconded one of my signalmen to be rapidly trained to join the barge's crew. Our seaman was taken to the local hospital and proved not to be seriously injured and, when repaired, would be sent rapidly home. How did we stop him telling the world? In those days, there was none of the blabbing to the media that haunts the military now. He was not charged with a homosexual act, which would have been difficult to prove as the other two participants maintained their silence. He was ordered to keep shtum.

As it turned out, the affair was quickly forgotten because the next day, King George VI died and Princess Elizabeth became Queen Elizabeth II and the tour was cancelled.

At 1512 hours on 6 February 1952, I received an 'Emergency' signal from the Admiralty in London:

> Telephone communications required now between
> General Browning and Horsley.

Browning was one of the King's top officials at Buckingham Palace and Horsley was the senior member of the royal household with the Princess. I feared the worst but had to keep absolutely silent. If

Horsley had been on board we could have connected him immediately by means of the high-powered telephone transmitter that had been specially installed for the tour. But he wasn't. He was up a tree in the national wildlife park with the Princess watching elephants, zebras and lions. I had to reach him urgently, but how? I had no idea whether there was a telephone dangling from the branches.

We had not been given a contact number for the royals' stay in the wildlife park because their stay was so short. I knew the site of the tree was near the Treetops Hotel, where you could watch the wildlife in some comfort. Did Kenya have a directory enquiries? I tried the local Mombasa exchange.

'Can you give me the number of the Treetops Hotel in the national wildlife park?'

'Where you say?'

'N-A-T-I-O-N-A-L W-I-L-D-L-I-F-E P-A-R-K, T-R-E-E-T-O-P-S H-O-T-E-L,' I repeated very clearly.

'OK, OK, I know, I will check.'

This was turning into a long delay before Princess Elizabeth could be told she was now Queen. At last the operator called back.

'Here is number.' I was quickly put through to the hotel.

'Is Mr Horsley there?'

'No, he is up the tree at Treetops.'

'Please send a runner at top speed and tell him there is an urgent telephone call for him.' There was another long delay before Horsley came on the line and I was able to tell him that General Browning wanted to speak to him most urgently. We heard no more and I presumed Horsley made contact with Buckingham Palace via the international telephone service from the hotel and was told that the King had died and he was to tell Prince Philip. We know that Philip broke the news to Princess Elizabeth. The next day, she flew home as Queen Elizabeth II. Thus the new reign was begun.

I had guessed the outcome but not the speed with which the tour was dismantled. Within forty-eight hours, the naval team was pitched out of *Gothic* and she was 'returned to trade', her brief moment of glory over until the following year when she took the Queen on her first major overseas tour to Australia and New Zealand and the Pacific

Islands. The naval team was split up and the communicators and I were allocated to a cargo ship, the SS *Drakensberg Castle*, which had room for some twenty passengers. Here ended my one and only royal tour.

Chapter 7

Ditched and Abandoned

I t was to be a slow, unglamorous journey home, quite the opposite of a royal tour, discharging cargo in various ports on the way.

Arriving on board SS *Drakensberg Castle* after the luxury of *Gothic* was a shock. There were no separate quarters for the officers – actually, only one officer, me. There was a communal lounge and bar, rather like a second-rate pub in Plymouth, and one small dining saloon. There were single cabins so I did not have to share. In those days in HM ships, the officers lived at one end of the ship and the ratings[1] lived up the other end. Officers and ratings lived strictly segregated social lives and only met on duty. So where could the one and only officer be accommodated in the style to which he was accustomed? He couldn't. I could hardly sit all day in my little sleeping cabin with meals being passed through the door as if I was in a prison cell. I supposed I could picnic on the upper deck. So, I decided, to hell with the class-conscious naval protocol, let's pretend we are all passengers on a Mediterranean cruise and muck in together. My communication ratings didn't seem to mind having me in their midst.

The removal from the glamour of a royal yacht to a humble cargo boat brought home to me that the glory days were over. At first I had been unsure of my role amidst the trappings of a royal tour. I had never mixed in that environment and was nervous as to whether I would perform properly in the demanding days that lay ahead. After the trial cruise out from the UK I had begun to look forward to the tour and to seeing at first-hand how this high-level style of living and performance worked out. It would have been exciting and glamorous and, hopefully, fun, the experience of a lifetime. It would have looked good on my CV. I might even have got an MVO (Member of the Victorian Order). Now we had been ditched and I felt abandoned. I had nothing to do and, from being quite an important person, I was a nobody. The loss of my fascinating appointment left me feeling depressed.

Thus it was that on a long, tedious journey home I abandoned my officer status and became one of the gang. It was the only time in my naval career that I lived amongst the sailors I commanded. They cheered me up and, thanks to them, my depression slowly lifted. They were an interesting bunch of young men, plus two delightful chief petty officers, and I enjoyed being taken on unusual 'runs ashore' in ports like Aden and Port Said, sampling a slightly different slice of life to the usual officer-like shore visits.

One particular run ashore that I will always remember was in Barcelona. A small group of us did the sights and then had a pleasant meal in a small café to vibrant music. Wine and music always sets me going and I joined a group dancing in the middle of the floor. They were mostly Spaniards, doing a fiery flamenco, and I performed what I thought was a truly dramatic dance. After a while I was the only male on the floor dancing with a young, dark-haired Spanish girl. There we were happily twirling around, thumping our thighs and stamping our feet in what I supposed was an excellent rendering of Spanish dance with the spectators clapping in rhythm to the music. Suddenly, one of my sailors tapped me on the shoulder and whispered, 'Sir, your partner's boyfriend has a knife and he is reputed to be very jealous. I think we should leave.'

I stopped dancing and turned round to see a scowling Spaniard looking daggers at me. I smiled weakly at him, bowed to my partner and mumbled, '*Buenas noches*,' before heading for the door with my gang behind me as a protective screen.

Thanks to the kindness and sensitivity of my crew I recovered my equanimity by the time we reached England and soon we were disembarking at Tilbury Docks. A lorry had come to pick us up and I decided to stick two fingers up at the world and wore the bowler hat bought solely to wear on the royal tour at the Melbourne Races in

Australia and have never worn since, except when dressing up at Christmas parties. I was decanted at Waterloo Station, where I said fond farewells to my team. One or two of them remained good friends beyond the confines of the Navy and we still visit each other to this day. It was an inglorious end to what might otherwise have been an amazing experience.

As I had been expected to be away for at least three months, the powers that be had to find a job for me to keep me out of trouble. During the war I had been a small cog in the ULTRA communications system. This organisation, based in Bletchley Park in Buckinghamshire, was staffed by the extremely clever civilians who succeeded in decoding the German ciphers and then translating the 'broken' signals into English and sending them out by radio in a special British cipher to commanders at sea and in the field. One of my wartime jobs at the Salerno and South of France landings had been to decode these British ciphers and present the results to my American admirals.

To work in the ULTRA system I had been comprehensively vetted during the war to make sure there was no murky political history in my background or any unsavoury incidents that might make me vulnerable to blackmail by Russian agents. Every year, I received the same letter from the Admiralty reminding me that on no account must I visit any countries within the Russian sphere – Poland, Hungary, Romania and so on. I suppose they thought I might be suborned by some communist houri who would lure me into her bed and extract top secrets from me. That might have been fun!

With this background I did not need to be vetted again and I was sent to Washington as part of a communications team representing the Government Communications Headquarters (a successor to Bletchley) and the Royal Navy in talks with the American Central Intelligence Agency. It was so secret that I cannot remember what it was all about, but it was most interesting to meet our American counterparts. The highlight of this visit was that I travelled out on the *Queen Mary* and back on the *Queen Elizabeth*, which submitted one to the extremes of luxury. This was a stark contrast to the squalor of my return journey from the abortive royal tour. I keep a menu of one of

ABANDON SHIP!

the dinners to remind me of the wonderful cuisine. There were eight courses.

If variety is the spice of life then the Navy scores high marks. In the previous few months I had prepared for a royal tour with the King, taken part in a top-secret mission to the United States and crossed the Atlantic both ways in the *Queens*. Now I waited for Their Lords of the Admiralty to tell me what they wanted me to do next.

Notes

1. In those days, the word 'ratings' included all those on the lower deck except petty officers and chief petty officers.

58

Chapter 8

Beached

After returning from Washington I was appointed to the Admiralty Signal and Radar Establishment (ASRE), a research facility perched on the top of Portsdown Hill above Portsmouth. It was primarily a civilian place, stacked with scientists who were researching the needs of the Navy for future radar and radio equipments.

Tacked onto the scientists were a number of naval officers who were called application officers and I was to be the Communications Applications Commander. It was an unsuitable job for me as my understanding of scientific matters was almost zero. The role of the applications officers was to clarify the Navy's needs for a particular piece of kit and advise the scientists whether the kit they were developing was practicable for a seagoing ship and, particularly, for handling by sailors less savvy than they were. You didn't really need a lot of scientific knowledge. The scientists provided that, but you did need to learn to ask the right questions and explain the peculiarities of ship operations. Would it fit into small ships' radio offices? Would simple sailors find it easy to operate? Perhaps I was suited for the job!

Work consisted of lots of meetings and discussions and it was totally unlike ship life. We clocked on by 9.00 am and left about 5.00 pm. As light relief I was asked if I would go undercover and work occasional weekends and evenings. The IRA had restarted their mainland bombing campaign and were attacking military and naval establishments. The naval counterterrorism unit wanted to test the security of naval shore establishments in the Portsmouth area and asked for volunteers to pose as civilian contractors, tradesmen or random members of the public and 'attack' a naval station. I decided to volunteer, to cheer up a rather dull existence. Our job was to get into a weapons store or some sensitive area and 'plant a bomb'. The bomb was a slip of paper that said, 'This represents an IRA 500lb bomb, which was placed on your desk at 1830, timed to go off at 2100.'

We usually left the bomb on some senior officer's desk and the idea was that he would immediately take measures to improve the security of the establishment. We also had to report to the counterterrorism unit what we had 'bombed'. To carry out the 'dangerous' task, I became a civilian electrician, employee of a mythical contracting company. I always operated alone, dressed in brown overalls and carrying my bag of tools. If anyone had asked me an electrical question I would have been floored.

I arranged to have some impressive but fraudulent passes printed to flourish at the gate sentries. Naval sentries ashore are hopeless; they never suspect anyone and are only too happy to have a bit of a chat and then direct you to your target. I managed to plant some bombs without being discovered but I didn't ever hear whether we succeeded in improving naval security. As there were no IRA attacks on the local naval establishments at the time, perhaps we did.

By this time I was beginning to be more useful at ASRE. I had learned that simple questions like 'how?' and 'what?', requiring answers that any fool like me could understand, were very effective in making clever scientists explain themselves clearly.

A major excitement in 1952 was the wedding of the first of my generation to get married, my younger brother, Michael, the one who had wrecked my wardrobe at my promotion party. I was to be his best man.

The country was still experiencing austerity after the war but we agreed we must have a stag party, though nothing like the extraordinary goings on that happen today. Nowadays, they take off for Morocco or Mexico and make fools of themselves on beaches or in a kasbah. In 1952, everything was much simpler and rather dull.

On the night before the wedding we took Michael out for his last taste of freedom before the bonds of marriage ensnared him. As best man I had to remain respectable. There wasn't much chance of any rip-roaring high jinks as we were accompanied by my uncle, Admiral Sir Gresham Nicholson, KBE, CB, DSO, DSC. In actual fact, although he was grand, he was great fun and had a mischievous sense of humour. The small party was completed by two of my brother's undergraduate friends from his Cambridge days.

After a pleasant dinner with a selection of wines, we were walking back to our hotel in Rugby with an élan that propelled us as if we were on air. The beauty of the leafy Rugby avenues did something to my dear uncle, who suddenly remarked, 'This road reminds me of the avenue of palm trees leading to Admiralty House in Ceylon.'

In 1944, Uncle had been the admiral responsible for the naval shore establishments on that island and lived in Admiralty House outside Colombo and both my brother and I had visited him there. We knew what he was talking about.

'Do you remember how the little monkeys shinned up the trees and threw baby coconuts down at passersby?' he added. So what followed was entirely his fault.

Foolishness is one of my weaknesses and this has led me into some stupidities, which now, in my advanced age, I prefer to forget. I have always liked climbing trees and it was obvious to me that Uncle was nostalgic for the glory wartime days in Ceylon. I felt I had to indulge him and it was also a golden opportunity to play the giddy goat, so I climbed up into the greenery of a nearby tree – an easy ascent. My young brother, spurred on by the example of his elder, also shinned up the next tree. Sitting on the lower branches we started throwing twigs at Uncle, while making squeaking monkey noises to simulate the scene in Ceylon that he had recalled. Uncle was convulsed with laughter. Then, out of the blue, Mr Plod appeared.

'What are you doing up there?' he politely enquired. Good question.

It was too difficult to explain about Ceylon, monkeys and admirals, so I pointed to my brother and said in a loud voice, 'We are getting married tomorrow.'

This floored him and he said, 'I think you had better come down.' I readily agreed and slithered down onto the pavement, somewhat dishevelled. As I descended, my uncle explained to the copper that my brother was getting married next day and that we had had a few, but he would see we got home without any further trouble. Splendid man, he understood perfectly.

'Go home and no more funny business,' he warned me. Certainly, officer, and three bags full, officer (not aloud).

Britain had still not fully recovered from the war and there wasn't much sparkle in these islands. Then, in the summer, of 1953, the country woke up in uninhibited revelry. The coronation of Queen Elizabeth II in June 1953 proved a welcome diversion from the greyness of daily living and parties were held all over the country. Like many others, our family decided to make the most of it.

On the day itself, my brother Michael and I, and some of our cousins who were brought up with us, met at 7.45 am on a cold, wet morning by the Serpentine in Hyde Park, with only one objective – to watch the processions and have a wonderful day. To help us enjoy the festivities we had each brought a bottle of hooch, with which we fortified ourselves before walking up Piccadilly, where we took up our positions opposite Green Park Station. Standing in a London crowd on ceremonial occasions is always hugely entertaining. Those around us became great buddies for the day, assisted by warming drinks and sandwiches and, on this very special day, good rations of alcohol, mostly provided by our family. We cheered the road sweepers; we cheered the police; we even cheered anyone who looked remotely regal as they passed on their way to the Abbey. Despite the rain, which persisted on and off all day, the crowd was good-humoured and excited and when the conquest of Mount Everest by Edmund Hilary and Sherpa Tensing was announced on the Tannoy, we gave the biggest cheer of all.

After the service in Westminster Abbey, which we listened to on the radio, Queen Elizabeth II's gilded coach came along Piccadilly and we had an excellent sight of her and Prince Philip as it came down the gentle slope towards Green Park. As the Queen passed us she looked radiantly happy, smiling broadly. She was so very young and beautiful. We felt we were entering a new Elizabethan era of achievement and success and leaving behind the dull, post-war years, although it didn't last long.

The procession of notables behind the Queen's coach was a fabulous sight and I can't imagine that we shall ever see such a pageant of glitter and glory again. This was a last fling for the dying British Empire. Representatives from all corners of the Empire paraded before us. In open landaus in the pouring rain, the governors general and prime ministers of the independent Commonwealth countries of Australia, New Zealand, Canada, India, Burma Pakistan, Ceylon and South Africa passed by and we gave them all a cheer. They were escorted by servicemen of their country who had fought in the Second World War on Britain's side. They were followed by the leaders of the Colonial Empire nearing independence, and a wonderful array of native soldiers, sailors and airmen marching by the side of their carriages. We toasted them in gin as they passed and roared a mighty cheer. Some of the servicemen from the tropical outposts looked absolutely miserable, drenched to the skin by the cold English rain.

The star of the parade was Queen Salote of Tonga, a massive 6-foot, 20-stone rock of a woman with a wide grin and perfect white teeth who repeatedly stood up erect in her carriage and waved her wand of office at the crowd. She seemed oblivious to the teeming rain running down the cleft in her massive bosom. I felt sorry for the wizened little man, sultan of somewhere, sitting opposite her, looking totally miserable. Queen Salote got the heartiest cheer of the lot.

It was a lengthy procession but on these occasions there are always distractions. Suddenly, I spied my old boss, Admiral Sir Rhoderick McGrigor, prancing along on a restless horse, looking distinctly unstable. Admirals, as a breed, are usually unused to horsemanship; seamanship is more in their line.

'Good luck,' I called as he passed, but he didn't hear me.

The procession took more than an hour to pass us. We were thrilled by the colour and music of the many military bands and catching our first glimpse of our radiant new queen. We were happy in more senses than one and despite the rain, we had a wonderful time.

After the parade we went down to Buckingham Palace to watch the Royal Family come out onto the balcony. There was a vast throng around the Palace and down The Mall. Somehow we got separated and I found myself alone in a surging mass cheering and shouting out, 'We want the Queen.' She came out alone onto the balcony to a mighty roar. Then Philip joined her. Repeatedly, the young couple came out and waved to us. It was a highly charged occasion. The crowd then flowed down to Embankment to watch a wonderful display of fireworks along the banks of the Thames. To round off the day I found myself on Westminster Bridge with a posse of Scots, including a piper, and we proceeded to dance the *Highland Fling* and a few other reels. We soon had several groups in the crowd dancing merrily. It was a splendid way to finish off an unforgettable day.

As I had to be at work next day, I managed to catch the last train to Portsmouth and get a few hours' sleep. It had been a nonstop party day and London had had a magnificent bash.

As ASRE was a scientific establishment there was no accommodation and no naval wardroom. We each had to find our own accommodation and, effectively, live a civilian life.

I don't know how it happened, but I found myself asked by a female acquaintance that I hardly knew to a dance in London. She must have been hard up for partners. When I got to a rather posh address in London I realised it was one of those 'debs' balls that young ladies attended after presentation at court. At that time, upper crust families would aim to have their daughters 'presented at court', which meant an evening soirée at Buckingham Palace, at which they queued up to walk past the Queen and make a low curtsey. After that they were deemed to have 'come out' and were available on the marriage market. The Queen abolished these presentations early in her reign.

Present at the dance were lots of young 'gels' and Guards officers much younger than my thirty-three years, and this made me realise my partner was either desperate or thought I was younger than I was. The ball was very decorous and not much fun and, to my horror, I was invited to another such ball two weeks later. I realised that my name had got onto some debs' ball list of 'suitable young men' who would not ravish their daughters. I rather suspect some of the daughters might have enjoyed a spot of ravishing. I turned the invitation down and was obviously, and thankfully, blacklisted as I was never asked again.

If my description of life at ASRE seems to be one long catalogue of amusements that have nothing to do with work it is simply that long lists of meetings and discussions about technical equipment that would only be fitted in the fleet many years ahead is not particularly fascinating to the lay reader. I tried to cheer up my bachelor existence with as many extramural excitements as possible.

I joined the RN Ski Club for a 1953 winter holiday in Austria. The party met one chilly January day at Victoria Station and we were to travel all the way to Innsbruck by train, crossing the Channel on the train ferry, which had railway lines along its hold so that the train could roll out at the French end. There was no air travel then. The money we were allowed to take abroad was limited to £50 each, so to preserve our funds for the nightlife of the ski resort we travelled third class, which consisted of wooden seats and no sleepers.

On arrival at Innsbruck, we changed into the coach for the climb up into the mountains at Sölden, where we boarded an overhead cable car to waft us up to Hochsölden (High Sölden) and our hotel. The cable car consisted of twin bucket seats open to the elements and suspended from an overhead wire, which threaded its way on pylons, passing through pine forests until it emerged on the upper snow-clad slopes at Hochsölden. With two in each open bucket seat we were soon swinging our way up into a starlit sky and we could just make out the mighty mountains towering above. It was hugely exhilarating, until we juddered to a halt. Looking down to the valley lights far below we wondered what was up. We hung there swaying gently in the freezing night, getting colder and colder. If we could have been assured of an early repair to the cable it would have been a magnificent moment. The glittering white Alps, star-studded sky overhead and crystal-clear atmosphere were breathtakingly beautiful. But no messages reached us and we had visions of either freezing to death where we sat or taking a perilous jump into the snow many feet below.

After what seemed like an eternity, but was probably only a quarter of an hour, we jolted forward and upward again and soon arrived at the lovely little unspoilt resort of Hochsölden. It was straight into our hotels and the welcoming warmth of strong, hot *gluhwein*. This was the start of a fabulous two weeks of perfect snow and sunshine, skiing all day and partying every evening. I don't know what it is about skiing, but however much you ski, you seem to have energy for dancing and drinking into the night. Not being a beginner, I joined a non-novice class and we had some wonderful mountain cross-country runs. As dusk fell, we returned to the hotel to watch the sun setting behind the Alps with the mountaintops, the Alpenglühen, turning from pink through mauve to ebony.

All too soon we were on our way back to work in a grey, post-war England.

After a year at ASRE, I felt a long way from the sea. This longing for the sea did not stop me enjoying the advantages of a shore life, with its complete freedom at weekends. It was the first time in my naval career that I had absolutely no weekend duties. So I was able to pick up again on one of my earliest enthusiasms, hillwalking. The family home was still on Dartmoor and when other social diversions allowed, I dashed off there in my ancient 'banger'.

I had first started walking on Dartmoor when I was fifteen and, with my younger brothers and cousins, we were holidaying at Lydford, on the western edge of the moor. I had recently been devastated when my mother told me that my father had deserted his family and would not be coming back again. He was in a ship in the Mediterranean. This news hit me hard and I felt the need to get away from everyone and everything and be totally alone. So occasionally I took off on my own into the desolate moor, climbed the great rocks of the tors and lost myself in the wilderness. From that time onwards, whenever I saw a hill or a tor I felt compelled to climb it. It was a strange compulsion that led me to many happy days and formed the beginning of a serious bug, climbing hills. Wherever I travelled in the world, if there was a hill to climb, I climbed it, from the Lake District or Scotland to Hong Kong and even Fujiyama, in Japan.

For me, there is nothing as uplifting as the quiet solitude when walking in the high hills. All around you, they are eternal, impassive and mysterious. The granite tors of Dartmoor have been there for thousands of years and will be there for thousands of years after I've gone; a salutary reminder of one's own insignificance. My young brother used to complain, when we dragged him out for walks on the moor, that it was bleak, cold and boring, without any of the beauties of woodland paths. But for me it's a feast of beauty. The moor's face is never still. As you stand on the summit of a tor you can see weather changes from afar and it's like looking at a series of paintings. The massive rocks, one instant lit up by sunlight, gleam like lighthouses, then turn almost black as the clouds roll over them. Jagged shadows steal up the valleys and slide across the hill slopes.

On a fine day, with the sun high above and a gentle breeze fluttering the white cotton grasses, with the skylarks high above singing their eternal song, I am near to heaven. Should one become over emotional, there is always a nearby pool in a swiftly running stream in which to cool off. On a hot summer's day, with no one in sight, it is a delight to submerge oneself in a deep river pool and feel the icy fingers of a waterfall cascade over your shoulders on its way to Plymouth Sound. So, whenever I had a free weekend, I took to the hills to revel in Dartmoor's delights, which was a kind of compensation for not being at sea.

Despite the diversions and distractions of free weekends, I was looking forward to escaping from this landlocked existence and sail out to sea again. As my time at ASRE neared its end, I was thrilled to be told that I was to have command of a destroyer on the Far East Station, based on Hong Kong. This was the most exciting news and exactly what I had been hoping for. It used to be every naval officer's dream to command a destroyer and it was also a favourable promotion. I had served in destroyers before and knew the life – much more informal than in the big ships and much more fun. I couldn't wait.

Chapter 9

HMS *Concord*

Working for two years amongst clever research scientists, adrift from the normal naval way of life in a ship at sea and amongst congenial messmates in the wardroom, had been an unfamiliar experience for me. It didn't suit me nor did I suit the job. I doubt if my contributions to research improved the equipment for the Navy of many years ahead but it had been useful trying to understand how the scientific mind worked and how research projects were organised, and some of the pitfalls of when a project became excessively elaborate and expensive. The Navy usually wanted more and better and the scientists were keen to oblige, but the result could end up over elaborate and way over budget. I was glad to escape back to the simplicity of life at sea. In the summer of 1954, I said goodbye to ASRE without any regrets.

Because I had been ashore for so long I was sent on command courses to ensure I was safe enough to be given a seagoing command. I studied tactics, navigation and seamanship and by November 1954, I was deemed fit to be let loose as captain of a destroyer. HMS *Concord* was one of six destroyers in the 8th Destroyer Squadron based on Hong Kong. There was also a cruiser squadron and a frigate squadron making up the Far East Fleet. *Concord* had been built during the Second World War and her bodywork was not of the highest quality; she rusted easily, but she was lovely to look at and was armed with eight 4.7-inch guns, eight torpedoes and numerous short–range anti-aircraft weapons.

Why was the Navy in the Far East? The Korean War had recently ended with the division of Korea into two halves; the northern half under a particularly tyrannical communist regime (which it still is) and the southern half 'free', but under American occupation. The Korean War, which lasted from 1950-53, had been fought under the banner of the United Nations (UN), the first and probably last such war. Backing the South Koreans was a large American army, a sizeable British force and contingents from Australia, New Zealand, South Africa, Turkey and other members of the UN. The North Koreans were supported by Russia and large numbers of the Chinese Army.

The war had been started when the communists in the north invaded the south and nearly occupied the whole of the Korean peninsula before the American forces in Japan, under the command of the famous General Macarthur, were despatched to reinforce the South Koreans. It had been a vicious war in which our army had achieved some glorious actions, such as the defiant stand against overwhelming odds by the Gloucestershire Regiment (the Glosters) on the Imjin River. It was also a war in which British National Servicemen, peacetime conscripts, were thrown into battle and were killed. The great British public by and large ignored this war. It was a forgotten, distant war but our casualties were far higher than in the more recent Iraqi and Afghan conflicts.

Concord had been active in the Korean War, bombarding shore batteries and supporting amphibious assaults by UN forces. During one such bombardment she had been hit by shore batteries and had suffered fatal casualties.

The war had ended in stalemate. The communist forces had been thrown out of the southern half of Korea but still retained their grip on the north and remained a threat to peace in South East Asia.

The other flashpoint was the island of Formosa, which had been taken over by General Chiang Kai-Shek, the Nationalist ruler of China who had been driven out of China by the forces of Mao Tse-tung, the Communist leader. Mao claimed Formosa as part of China. The Americans and British did not recognise China's claim and supported an independent Formosa. To give backing to this, the British had the sizeable Far East Fleet and we kept a single destroyer on patrol in the Formosa Straits between the mainland and the island as a 'lookout' to report any signs of a Chinese invasion force. The

Americans maintained much larger forces based in Japan and on the island of Okinawa.

Concord's mission was to take its share of the Formosa Straits patrol; to exercise with the United States Navy to preserve our Anglo-American capability and to show the flag in Japan. We were also required to assist the first British atom bomb trials team on the Monte Bello Islands off the western coast of Australia.

Command of Her Majesty's Ships is a unique experience and the first command is particularly challenging and daunting, but also exciting and fulfilling. A captain is totally responsible for everything that happens on board and for every person in the ship. The safety of the ship is paramount, as is the safety of each member of the crew.

The relationship between a captain and his officers and the crew is complex. They depend on his judgement and fairness in disciplinary matters and on his personal skills in handling his ship under all conditions of weather and in her safe navigation in congested harbours and coastal waters. He depends on the collective skills of his officers and crew to run the ship efficiently in harbour and at sea.

If he wins their respect he will get all the support he needs to run his ship efficiently. His officers, chief petty officers and petty officers will all help him but if things go wrong, he and he alone carries the can. If he runs his ship aground or hits another vessel he will be held responsible even if he is not on the bridge at the time. It is a hard but excellent discipline.

But I am getting ahead of myself as my crew and I are still at Stanstead Airport on a very cold, damp November day, waiting for our flight to be called. Because we had to overfly neutral countries such as Turkey, we were not allowed to travel in uniform so an array of plain, civilian clothes in the terminal made it difficult to see who my future officers were and who the sailors were. The latter, seamen and stokers, knew at once who to avoid: they could smell an officer a mile away and they kept well clear of me.

We were being subjected to one of the earliest commissioning of a ship by air instead of by sea. Up to 1954, crews commissioning ships in the Far East enjoyed a leisurely cruise in a troop ship, gradually acclimatising to the heat of the tropics and getting to know each other.

We were the guinea pigs for commissioning by air. In 1954, air travel was slow by comparison with the twenty-first century. Our first night stopover was in Cyprus, the next in Bahrain, then Karachi and Calcutta before finally arriving in Singapore. Five days' travel and four uncomfortable nights in the low-grade hotels that the Admiralty felt we were entitled to.

I arrived in Singapore jetlagged and exhausted to find myself in a steam bath. The Singapore climate is tropical and humid and drains your energy. There was no let-up. We were bussed straight to the dockyard, where HMS *Concord* was lying alongside the jetty in the Singapore Naval Base. As I stepped off the bus from the airport, my beautiful destroyer, slim and powerful, lay stretched along the jetty, the first ship under my command as captain.

I gazed at her and thoughts tumbled through my mind. She would shortly be my responsibility and should we ever have to fight, the efficiency of her weapons and her warlike capability would be down to me. Together with the ship's company we would have to work up that fighting effectiveness so that *Concord* was ready for any challenge. We might be required to bombard enemy positions ashore, attack shipping with our torpedoes and guns and defend ourselves against air attack.

Command in the Royal Navy is a tremendous privilege, but also a weighty burden. A new captain has many helpers but he lives an isolated life in his own quarters. I had been the second-in-command during the war for nearly two years but there is no comparison between being the first and being the second. The latter always has the protective shield of his captain.

I paused for a moment on the dockside, looked my ship up and down and wondered what the coming months would unveil. The first command is the climax of a naval officer's career, the sought-after Holy Grail. Would I rise to the challenge? Would I run the ship on the rocks? Would I handle the officers and the crew sensibly? Would I be tough enough? Would I lead the ship's company to make *Concord* a really efficient fighting ship and, perhaps, a happy one.

Fleeting thoughts before going up the gangway to salute the quarterdeck and meet my predecessor, Kit James, an old friend of mine who had been my cadet captain (prefect) at Dartmouth and who had inflicted three 'cuts' of the cane on my bum for some minor misdemeanour. I bore him no malice.

The Navy doesn't make much fuss when handing over the command of a ship worth several millions. The incoming captain checks the confidential and secret books and documents against the register, counts the money in the contingency fund, and that's it.

'It's all yours. Good luck,' from my predecessor and, after some reminiscences of the past, Kit James left the ship. Back in my cabin I sat down for a few moments of calm. She was all mine now, the goal for which the seven years of training at Dartmouth and as a midshipman and later experience had prepared me. Challenges still lay ahead and in my mind there was a small cloud of doubt. A knock on the door soon put an end to my useless musings.

'The ship's company are fallen in on the quarterdeck, Sir,' the First Lieutenant reported. I walked aft for my first words to the ship's company. There would be many more as I believed in always keeping them informed about our plans. I looked them over and 200 pairs of eyes checked me out, thinking this is our skipper and wondering what he'll be like. I kept it short. This was only an introduction so that they could recognise their captain in future.

'Ship's company, right turn, dismiss,' and away they went to their mess decks.

Preliminaries completed, the First Lieutenant invited me to the wardroom for a less formal get-together with the officers, whom I would see individually after lunch. After that I would walk round the ship on my own and assess her condition. The rest of the day saw me secluded in my cabin reading the Eastern Fleet Orders, the 8th Destroyer Squadron Orders and numerous other relevant documents about life on the China Station. We were off.

It had been an ordeal to leave England in the freezing cold and travel some 12,000 miles by air and land, arrive in the heat of Singapore and commission a ship with a completely new ship's company within a matter of hours. As a result of our experiences I wrote a stinging report on 'Air Commissioning', and future crews were sent to a rest camp in Singapore for a couple of days to acclimatise. We had no time for such luxuries as we were immediately required to support our troops fighting the communist insurgents in what was called the Malayan Emergency.

After the Second World War, Soviet Russia tried to export communism wherever it detected a weakness in a capitalist area. This was what Marx had called the World Revolution and was one of the central pillars of communism. Russia had succeeded to some extent in Europe.

During the war in the Far East we had supported a number of communist underground groups fighting the Japanese in Malaya and Sumatra. After lying low for a number of years and reinforced by others infiltrating from the north, these groups started a campaign of murder and mayhem directed at the mainly British rubber planters and tin mining operations in Malaya, which then depended heavily on rubber and tin for its prosperity.

Concord's first task was to bombard an area of jungle where a group of communists was suspected of having infiltrated and set up camp. The next morning we sailed to bombard the enemy. The first time a captain takes his ship out of harbour is a testing experience as he does not yet know her capabilities. He knows the crew are watching him and the critical eyes of his officers will be assessing his ship-handling skills. The engine room staff will be counting the number of times he orders changes to the engine revolutions. A smooth, well-controlled manoeuvre means few changes of revolutions that control the ship's speed. It is a black mark if he has to order full-speed astern as it probably arises from a misjudgement. The sailors on the upper deck are hoping he will not scrape the ship's side, necessitating repainting. Everyone is watching him.

On our first exit from the dockyard we had to go out of the dock backwards (astern) and I then had to swing the ship's stern upstream through 90 degrees so as to point the bows downriver towards the open sea, like reversing a car into a narrow opening. The channel to the open sea is a long, narrow country lane of about 12 miles. Weary after our five days' flight, it was an ordeal of intense concentration.

I had an excellent navigator to help me, Jeremy Grindle, who is still a good friend. Also on the bridge was Midshipman Andrew Rowe, later the MP for Sevenoaks and Chief Yeoman of Signals, Stew. Somehow we got safely away to the ocean. The chief yeoman whispered to me, 'Very good, Sir,' which was kind but unexpected.

We steamed fast to our bombarding position and anchored a couple of miles offshore, because a ship can bombard more accurately from a static position. In front of us, sandy beaches stretched for miles, backed by thick jungle trees spreading inland and along the coastline like a vast green ocean. It was far too dangerous to risk landing bathing parties, due both to the sharks and the Chinese insurgents.

The army signalled us the area we were to bombard – not a pinpoint bombardment, more a general frightener. We were required to fire one shell a minute from our forward 4.7-inch gun, which is the main armament of a destroyer. There was little for me to do once we had anchored and the first rounds were seen to be in the target area. The communists had no big guns to threaten us with and I was able to get some rest, which was disturbed every minute as the forward gun went off just in front of my cabin. By then I was so tired I managed to sleep through it. After several days of rather fruitless bombardment, we returned to Singapore and shortly afterwards sailed to Hong Kong to start our 'work-up'.

Every newly commissioned ship has to work up, exercising all systems and weapons and every piece of machinery. Each man has to be trained in his action station, his battle position. The fire fighters, the leak pluggers, the boiler and engine room crews, the command team in the operations centre – all have to be put through their paces until what had once been a disorganised mishmash becomes a highly efficient team ready for every challenge.

A ship is a confined space, a steel box within which 200 men live, eat and sleep. The ship has to be kept scrupulously clean and so do the crew. In those days, the lower deck ratings slept and ate in one space, their mess deck. Each section of the crew – seamen, engineers, communications ratings, Chinese cooks and stewards – had their own mess deck, usually about twenty men to a mess. A central galley (kitchen) cooked the food and the so-called 'cook of the mess' collected it and dished it out on the mess deck at meal times.

ABANDON SHIP!

At night, each rating slung his hammock, just like I had done when I was a midshipman, above the dining table and wherever there was a space and slept there. Officers slept in double or single cabins and ate in the wardroom, where there was a bar, open in harbour, and where they also socialised. The wardroom was the centre of their off-duty activities. The captain's suite consisted of a small sleeping cabin, a shower cubicle, and a spacious day cabin that combined office, dining room and sitting room, which was where he entertained.

When you assume command it means a huge change to your lifestyle. Whereas once I had been a member of the gang of young officers in the wardroom of all my previous ships, with several good friends to go with for a run ashore and to make merry, as captain, I was required to live a life of monastic loneliness while on board. I lived, fed and slept alone, confined to my cabin in splendid isolation. I was only expected to mingle socially with my officers in the wardroom when they invited me, which wasn't too often. They didn't really want me listening to the antics they got up to ashore. Only on rare and special occasions would I go with them for a run ashore. This was the naval tradition in 1955. This austere captain's lifestyle was also intended to protect the aura that is supposed to surround the command and prevent him becoming overfamiliar with his juniors. For a comparatively young and social 36-year-old it all seemed a trifle heavy, but I knew my place.

However, I was still human. So how could I let my hair down? With an occasional run ashore with other captains in the squadron or old friends on other ships: a jolly meal in a local restaurant with a few bottles of wine and good chat and then back on board to my solitary bunk.

After one such an evening ashore I was returning to *Concord*, walking through the dockyard with my friends, enjoying the cool of the evening, when I noticed a huge pile of wooden baulks that are used as vertical supports for jetties, each one 15-20 feet long. Now I have always been a keen amateur historian and when my inner parts have been well lubricated with wine, the imagination is apt to flower. This pile of wood reminded me of one of the great events of British history, the capture of Quebec in Canada from the French in 1759.

In case you don't know the story, the French army occupied a heavily fortified Quebec, high above the St Lawrence River on the Heights of Abraham. On the river side the city was protected by steep cliffs, considered by the French to be impregnable. The British Commander, General Wolfe, reckoned he could find a way up these heights and surprise the enemy, which he did, and defeated the French and won Quebec. As a result, the whole of Canada became British, but Wolfe was killed in the hour of victory.

I imagined that the pile of timber, about 20 feet high, represented the Heights of Abraham, leading to Quebec and I started climbing up it, calling to my astonished friends below: 'Follow me; I am General Wolfe and we will surprise the French and take Quebec.' I clambered to the top of the pile and looked down and, of course, it wasn't Quebec; instead there was a Hong Kong dockyard policeman looking up at me.

'What you do up there?' he asked politely.

'I am General Wolfe and I have just captured Quebec for the British Empire.'

He didn't seem impressed. No sense of humour.

'I tink you better come down here.'

By now I thought so, too. As I turned to climb down I spied my mates skulking behind a large drum of cable wire laughing their heads off, hoping to see me marched off to the police station.

Dockyard policemen the world over are used to the antics of naval officers and ratings and he merely said, 'I tink you better go back on board.'

I readily agreed, apologised and collected my friends for a nightcap. Being my first command I took my responsibilities desperately seriously. Dignified and rather pompous, at thirty-six I was probably very stuffy and, of course, elderly, when many of my officers were ten years younger.

On board ship I could marry couples, commit a corpse to the deep, hold church services, which I did every Sunday, and imprison wrongdoers for up to six months in the naval detention quarters. I was as close to being a deity as I will ever get in this world, or any other.

ABANDON SHIP!

At this time Hong Kong was a wonderful station for the Navy. The locals were very welcoming and the colony seemed politically content, though the inhabitants had little say in their governance, which can be summed up as 'benevolent paternalism'. It was the Navy that originally occupied Hong Kong when it was uninhabited, except for a small fishing village on Victoria Island. China had been forced to cede the Hong Kong territories in 1843 under the terms of the Treaty of Nanking, after the end of the first Opium War.

There had been two Opium Wars from 1839-42 and 1856-60, due to British merchants from India plying a lucrative trade importing opium into China. Opium was a prohibited drug in China and the Chinese government tried to stop its importation. Open warfare broke out in 1839, when Britain objected to the Chinese treatment of the British merchants in Chinese ports when they tried to stop them unloading their lethal cargo. As a result of these wars we forced China to tolerate the opium trade and to open their ports to unrestricted foreign trade. Opium flooded into China and caused much addiction, and their defeat in these two wars rankled with Chinese governments and still does. It was not the most glorious incident in British history.

Now Hong Kong was a teeming city, spread along the coast of Victoria Island and on the opposite Kowloon shore on the mainland. The streets were like canyons with high-rise apartments soaring up into the sky and heaps of washing hanging on long poles from balconies above the streets. The houses of the colonial masters and the wealthy Taipans[1] spread up the steep hillside to the top of the ridge, known as the Peak, where I had lived in 1921-23 when my father was serving in the China Squadron in HMS *Hawkins* and where my elder brother had died at the age of five.

In harbour there were excellent sporting facilities located inside the Happy Valley racecourse circuit, which was somewhat bizarre as you might be playing hockey with race horses exercising all round you. It was a magnificent setting for the sports pitches in a bowl surrounded on three sides by the peaks of Victoria Island rising steeply above the racecourse. Playing football or hockey or any other team game was one of the few opportunities for all ranks to get together and for rank to be temporarily forgotten. I played hockey for the ship and over a drink afterwards I could get to know some of our sailors better, and perhaps they appreciated that I was more normal than they thought.

High up on one of the hills above the racecourse my 5-year-old brother lay buried in the Anglican cemetery. In 1922, just before Christmas, he had been rushed into the naval hospital to be operated on for appendicitis but it was too late and he died of peritonitis on 22 December. Soon after we arrived in Hong Kong I decided to look for his burial place. I found it in the furthest corner of the cemetery, high up on the remote hillside. Such a tiny little grave with a simple cross leaning at an angle, untended for over thirty years.

> Patrick Robert McCrum
> 17th April 1917- 22nd December 1922
> Elder son of Lieutenant Cecil McCrum, Royal Navy
> and Ivy McCrum
> Rest in Peace

I thought of the agony of my parents at losing their elder son so young. I stayed there for some time and then walked back down the hill and through the teeming streets to my ship in thrall to the memory of my brother.

Very occasionally in harbour when we had no duties I liked to take off and get away from the ship and the Navy and walk in the hills on one of the more sparsely populated islands, of which there were many scattered around the approaches to Hong Kong. Once you reached these islands there were green hills and valleys, much like the west coast of Scotland, and a welcome tranquillity.

One such weekend with our electrical officer, Bill Hunter, who came from the west coast of Scotland, we took the ferry to Lan Tao, one of the larger of these islands. Since then it has had the tops of its peaks sliced off for a runway that was built for the new international airport. We landed on a rickety jetty in a little bay on the island's north side. As we walked inland we quickly came upon a tumbling stream, rock-strewn and mossy, which was exactly like a Scottish burn. We followed a rocky path to the top of a steep hill and emerged into cultivated rice fields surrounding a Buddhist monastery, built on a plateau at the summit.

We decided to pay the monks a call and they welcomed us and sat us down and brought cups of tea and delicious little cakes. They sat with us as we drank and with their understanding of a few words of English we explained who we were and thanked them for their hospitality, whereupon they suggested we stay the night. It was early evening and we decided to stay. I had no Sunday duties as the ship was having a self-maintenance period, a sort of nautical MOT. After a light supper we were shown to a small cell with two bunk beds on hard boards and given a blanket each. After the exertion of our climb we slept well and when we woke the monks gave us a healthy breakfast and invited us to attend the Buddhist Early Morning Service. This was attended by all the monks and, to my surprise, some nuns. The service was reminiscent of a Roman Catholic mass with lots of incense being chucked about and much chanting of prayers. It was an intensely spiritual experience and reinforced my belief that Christianity was not the only valid religion.

After prayers we bade farewell to the monks and walked the length of the island to catch another ferry back to Hong Kong. It had been a memorable and restorative weekend for me. I wonder what happened to the monastery when the airport was built.

We spent many days at sea on the Formosa Straits Patrol. I never thought our patrols had much point as the Americans kept a much closer watch on Formosa. I suspected it was to give us something to do. It also gave me the chance to train the officers of the watch on the bridge in dealing with emergencies. To liven up the long days of patrolling I would arrive unexpectedly on the bridge and shout: 'Man overboard – for exercise' and throw a lifebelt over the side to represent the drowning sailor. I then watched to see how skilfully the officer of the watch manoeuvred the ship and how speedily the lifeboat was lowered into the water. There were several little ploys like that to keep everyone on their toes.

'Fire in the galley flat.'

'Stand by to take damaged ship in tow.'

Apart from these diversions the patrols were dull and boring and we never had anything interesting to report. I certainly enjoyed being out in the open sea again. In those days we still had bridges open to the weather and the sky and the ocean. If you are fascinated by the marvels of nature, the constant changes of the wind and the clouds on the face of the sea are wonderful to behold. Dawn slowly rising out of the distant horizon transforms the surrounding ocean into a blood-red lake and then it slowly melts away into green sea. With the twilight, the horizon quickly vanishes in the tropical night and the stars shine as bright as diamonds in a black sky. The effects of nature are seldom the same one day to the next and I never tired of being at sea. It was also the natural element for the ship and it gave me the same sort of pleasure as walking in the hills of Dartmoor.

In addition to the ships on patrol there was always a second ship in Hong Kong harbour designated as 'emergency destroyer', which meant she had to be ready to sail at short notice to go to sea to rescue sinking fishing boats or larger vessels and passengers from crashed aircraft. Only limited shore leave was allowed when we were on emergency duties.

One night at about midnight when we were emergency destroyer, I received a signal:

> *Concord* from Commodore Hong Kong.
> Aircraft reported crashed in Formosa Straits in
> position ... north ... east. Proceed to investigate at
> best speed.

The naval shore patrols rounded up as many of the men on leave as they could find in the pubs and brothels and we had enough crew to set out. Hong Kong harbour is never peaceful; day and night it is a hive of activity. Large merchant ships at anchor fill the channel and cross channel ferries from Victoria to Kowloon on the mainland run all night. I reversed the ship out of the dockyard basin and headed downstream. Due to the emergency I was going a little faster than normal in such a crowded anchorage. To my horror a cross channel Star ferry suddenly appeared from behind the bows of a large merchant ship, moored in the channel, only a few yards from *Concord's* bows. We were heading straight for her and she was crowded with passengers, a hundred or more. I ordered 'Full Speed Astern' to the engine room and rang down to tell them it was an emergency order. Slowly our speed was checked and we juddered to a halt, missing the ferry by a few feet. Had we hit her she would have been rolled over and capsized and few of the non-swimming Chinese passengers would have escaped. It would have been a major disaster. The irony of the situation was that the call-out proved to be a false alarm. There was no crashed aircraft and after searching for a few fruitless hours we were ordered to return to harbour.

When in harbour social life was hectic. I threw dinner parties and cocktail parties for local friends and my own officers. I was fortunate in having excellent Chinese supporting staff of cooks and stewards. Almost a quarter of our crew, laundrymen, cooks and stewards were local Chinese. They were a wonderfully hardworking bunch and very loyal to the Navy. It was considered a privilege to be 'a locally entered Chinese naval rating' and by Hong Kong standards their pay was high. I often wondered what they really thought about their life on board and about us, these odd naval types. Did they resent their colonial masters? They are an inscrutable race and I never really knew what they were thinking.

We had been 'on station' about six months and the dreaded Captain (Destroyers) Inspection descended on us. This usually occurred once a commission, unless you failed, and then you had to do a 'resit'. This was our first trial. The captain commanding the 8th Destroyer Squadron came on board with his staff, who were also 'inspectors'. The day of misery started with an inspection of every compartment for cleanliness and neatness. Where the Captain did not go, his staff would go, down to the storerooms and magazines in the bowels of the ship. Nothing escaped their eagle eyes.

After that, mayhem began. This was called General Drill and you had to be prepared for anything the captain and his staff threw at you.

'Boarding Party fall in on the quarterdeck.' This was our anti-piracy platoon with all their equipment.

'Let go second anchor.'

'Stand by to take stricken ship in tow,' and so on.

If he had a sense of humour, and ours did, there would be some funnies.

'Midshipmen man the motor boat. Proceed to HMS ... Calculate the average age of the midshipmen there and semaphore the result back to the ship.'

'What is the height of Kilimanjaro?'

'Make an omelette *a l'espagnol* – to test the chef's cooking and French.

By the end of the morning the ship looked like a dockyard after a hurricane. Ropes and wires unreeled, criss-crossing the decks, and bits of equipment strewn around. Sheer bedlam, but that was only the beginning.

The next day was at sea – the more important part of the inspection. Action stations were exercised and shooting at targets tested the gunnery. During these exercises damage and casualties were simulated.

'Steering gear breakdown, steer by hand.'

'The bridge has been hit by a shell. The captain is dead and the officer of the watch is severely wounded.'

This would reveal whether I had trained the officers satisfactorily to take over my responsibilities. This let me out and it was quite a relief to sit back and enjoy the mayhem. By the time the ship returned to harbour after her two days' inspection everyone was totally frazzled and in the evening post mortem in the wardroom we retold tales of near disaster and chaos and had a great celebration that it was all over. I was surprised a week later to receive a mainly favourable report with many suggestions for further improvements. We would try.

Much of our seagoing time was spent exercising with the rest of the Far East Fleet. Although it was peacetime we had to keep our skills in gunnery, torpedo attacks and damage control well honed. There was the constant threat of war between China and Taiwan, with the Americans supporting Taiwan and we expected to be dragged in on the US Navy's coat-tails.

From time to time, we also exercised with the United States Navy Pacific Fleet. We were a very small component of that vast array of warships and it was excellent experience to work with such a huge force. We hunted submarines, we screened the large aircraft carriers, we fought off air attacks and carried out day and night torpedo attacks on the battleships. It taught me a lot and gave me my first experience of being at sea in a large fleet and for long enough to have to refuel the ship from an oil tanker at sea. Steaming along 50 feet apart from a large oil tanker at 15 knots called for close concentration and it was good training for officers of the watch, with me watching anxiously and ready to intervene if disaster looked imminent.

After one such exercise we were sent on a showing the flag visit to Japan and we were ordered to visit the capital, Tokyo, which tested my courtesy as I still recalled the skeletal prisoners of war we had rescued from Changi prisoner of war camp in Singapore at the end of the war in 1945 in HMS *Tartar*. On arrival, all the ships had issued an open invitation to the newly-released servicemen to come on board and enjoy our hospitality. I could never forget those walking skeletons, who just wanted to sit and talk as they had had no news since their capture by the Japs. They told us grisly stories of prisoners being decapitated in public for minor offences and of their starvation.

Amongst various ceremonies, I had to make an official call on the Mayor of Tokyo, who seemed to spend a lot of the time bowing at me. The Japanese are keen on bowing and I felt that for the sake of Britain I should reciprocate, but I couldn't get out of my mind the terrible treatment meted out to our prisoners by the Japanese military and never felt comfortable during this visit.

To get away from the many entertainments for a couple of days I had an idea that it might be fun to take a party to climb Fujiyama, the extinct volcano near Tokyo (12,000 feet). I had read somewhere that before one dies one should watch the sun rise over Tokyo Bay from the summit of Fujiyama. I suggested to the ship's company that some of them might like to climb Fuji with me.

By this stage of our commission the sailors were somewhat chary of their captain's batty ideas. Nevertheless, some fifteen volunteers set out by coach to take us to the rest house, which was about halfway up the mountain and where we had a Japanese supper before starting the climb at dusk. It was too hot to climb it in the heat of the day and we climbed through the night.

It was not a pleasant climb, just a steep walk, mostly over volcanic cinders. Each foot forward resulted in half a pace backwards as the cinders gave way beneath your feet. The climb was spoilt for me when, nearing the summit, I suffered a bout of mountain sickness. Giddiness and violent nausea hit me and made the last few hundred feet purgatory. The side of the mountain seemed to move and sway as if one was drunk and I found it difficult to make progress. I wasn't the only one to suffer. A kind sailor hauled me up the last slope and I did get to the top. It had been quite a long and steep climb and we ought to have taken things more slowly to become acclimatised but we didn't have the time. I recovered enough to watch the sun rise over Tokyo Bay and light up the sea in pink and gold. It was a memorable occasion and worth the struggle.

Scrambling down the cinder track was easy and we ran all the way to the rest house, where we had an excellent breakfast before bussing back to the ship.

Our next stop was Kure, a naval base on the Inland Sea. As well as being a Japanese naval base, Kure was also at that time a US Navy Pacific Fleet port. The Inland Sea runs for over 200 miles with one entrance at the south end and another at the north-east end. It varies in width from 40 miles to a few hundred yards. It's a spectacular stretch of sea enclosed by the islands of Kyushu, Shikoku and the Japanese mainland. Because of its sheltered waters we decided it would be fun to aquaplane, being towed by the ship – a rather unusual sport for a destroyer. An aquaplane is simply a wooden platform, curved at the front, about 3 feet wide and 6 feet long, with a towing bar hitched to a tow rope leading from the ship. Standing at the rear end of the plane and clutching the tow rope it was exhilarating to swing the plane around. I settled the ship on a speed of 12 knots and left the officer of the watch in charge. I then climbed over the stern and 'had a go' to test all systems. It was most exciting to be towed along behind my ship with the hills of the islands rising on either side and appearing so close. There were many volunteer aquaplaners and we carried on for at least 60 miles until we were approaching the entrance to Kure Bay.

One of the experiences that is unique to Japan is a visit to a tea house. In naval ports, tea houses usually have a bath house attached, and some have a brothel, which gives the seafarer a three-pronged choice. After we had docked it was one of the rare occasions that I was invited to go ashore with the wardroom.

'A visit to a Japanese tea house, Sir. Would you like to come?'

It seemed harmless, so I said yes.

A group of about six of us taxied to a well-known tea house in the evening. The tea ceremony was totally stylised. Little cups of tea and cakes are offered round by the hostesses, or geishas, dressed in the national dress, the kimono. There was much bowing and rather artificial smiling and they engaged one in rather stilted conversation as they had only a few words of English.

'You like Japan?' 'Where you from?' and so on. It wasn't particularly stimulating but this was really the warm-up before visiting the bath house.

'You like me wash you?'

OK, I'll have a go!

The bath was a huge tub about 5 feet deep in which you stood or sat on the bench and the hostess washed and massaged your upper works. I wasn't sure I wanted her messing about on the lower parts so I indicated that I would deal with those myself. Then you were dried off in a sauna. It was extraordinarily relaxing. After the bath there were two options. If you turned left you entered a brothel with multi-choice products: if you turned right you went back to the tea room and drank expensive beer and made small talk sitting on the floor in a kimono. Being about to get married, I turned right and probably spoilt the evening for some of my officers as they felt they had to follow my example. It was certainly an experience but once was enough.

The visit to Japan had been interesting but not enjoyable. There were too many ghosts and I was glad to get back to Hong Kong.

Notes

1. A Taipan was a wealthy businessman, banker or trader.

Chapter 10

Wedding Bells

After the interest and excitements of 'working up' the ship it had dawned on me that I would not see Angela, my future wife, for nearly two years. We would then both be thirty-eight.

I had met Angela nine years earlier, in 1946, in that bruising encounter about the lack of a telephone in my office at Plymouth. A few weeks later, she became my assistant for a short time before departing abroad. No flames were lit at that time. I had only just recovered from the sad ending of a fond relationship and wasn't looking for anything more permanent than brief encounters.

Three years later, we met up at the Signal School and I thought what a nice person she was but again, fate intervened, as I was heavily involved with someone else at that time. Angela then departed to Malta and nearly married a Royal Marine officer, but this fighting soldier was cowed by his mother, who flew out to Malta and made him break off the engagement because she didn't approve of him marrying a Wren officer five years older than he was. What a wimp.

When Angela returned from Malta she went back to the Signal School and we met again, both of us free of entanglements, and we became close but I had not popped the question.

Why was I so reluctant? Why had I jibbed at marriage several times in my life, causing pain to people of whom I was very fond?

Whenever a relationship became really serious a dark shadow loomed up behind me and a strong arm gripped my shoulder and turned me away. That unseen presence had held me in thrall for many years. More than once I had failed a girl I loved at the last moment and once, in one of my lifetime's most embarrassing moments, I was asked directly if I intended marriage. I didn't. I just thought we were having fun. Oh, the shame!

Marriage had been an abysmal failure in the McCrum family. For three generations no male McCrum had fulfilled a lifetime's marriage. My grandfather was divorced by his Canadian wife and never married again. My great-grandfather lost his wife to tuberculosis at the age of twenty-nine and never remarried. My father went to a ship in the Mediterranean and never came back. He left his wife and family for a more up-to-date model and never told me why. I was fifteen at the time and was devastated to be abandoned by someone I loved and whom I thought loved me. His desertion affected me and my two brothers for our entire lives. I only saw my father three times during the following forty years.

McCrum and marriage did not seem to go together and I was utterly determined that if I got married it would be successful both for us and our children. Both the heart and the head needed to be certain.

When I realised that I would not see Angela again for a long time I decided to face my demons and ask her to marry me. At last, the restraining hand on my shoulder loosened its grip and I proposed to her by letter.

By this time, Angela held a senior appointment in charge of all the Wrens at a naval air station and by the rules that then prevailed she was immediately required to resign her commission as a Wren officer and give up her job if she wanted to get married. There was no pension, even after fifteen years, including four years of war service. Bravely, she flew out alone to join me in Singapore, where my ship was refitting in the dockyard. Long-distance air travel was in its infancy and none of our families were able to fly out for the wedding so we did not have to endure the fuss that some families make of these occasions. We had to organise the nuptials without their help. It might have seemed selfish to marry abroad but we felt the pressures of age and wanted to waste no further time.

We were to be married in the dockyard church, not the cathedral, as our mothers might have wished. I wasn't fussy, nor was Angela. At that time I was a paid-up agnostic as far as religion was concerned, but I did believe in making my marriage vows in a serious setting and church seemed as fitting as any. Angela, a truly believing Christian, would have been devastated if we had not married in church. We chose the dockyard church for its simplicity.

As I sat in the customary front pew waiting for my bride, I looked around at that simple little church. It was as if we were being married in a garden. The only walls were at the two ends, the east behind the altar and the west end at the back of the church. To allow the breeze to cool the tropical heat, the two long sides were open to the gardens and the sky. Somehow, these natural surroundings seemed just right.

Behind me, almost my entire ship's company had turned up, a sea of crisp, white tropical uniforms. I was greatly touched but I expect it was really the prospect of beer afterwards that brought them.

A lovely bride walked slowly towards me and the service began. Those wonderful words, 'Will you take ... to be your lawful wedded wife, to have and to hold until death do you part.'

'I will.' And I did, until death did us part.

As we repeated our vows after the priest I became suffused with a sense of awe and complete acceptance. I might not have believed in God any more but these vows were now sacred to me and, despite my disbelief, as strong, even stronger, than a purely Christian promise. This was real to me and binding, forever.

It was a transformation and, as we stepped out of church under the traditional arch of naval swords into the searing heat of a tropical day, I felt complete.

We left the church for two receptions. The ship's company were all invited to a reception in the Royal Navy club for sandwiches and as much beer as they could consume. Personal friends were entertained in the officers' shore mess. We oscillated happily between the officers' mess and the RN club, where the sailors consumed icebergs of beer and gave us an uproarious welcome. At the more sedate officers' mess we drank champagne and listened to mercifully short speeches; there were no friends of the family to tell risqué stories of mine or the bride's early days. Just as well.

From a scrap heap I had bought a Morris Tourer for our honeymoon. I had booked us in at a hill resort called Fraser's Heights,

89

where it was cool and I thought Angela would enjoy a respite from the heat.

At this time the Malayan Emergency was still going and parts of the country were declared 'black zones', indicating that in these areas there was a possible danger of armed attack by communist guerrillas. We were allowed to drive through such zones but not to stop for any reason. To get to Fraser's Heights we had to drive through one black zone for about an hour. This was the hour the car chose to break down comprehensively in the middle of a rubber plantation. We juddered to a halt and nothing would move the animal. I imagined little yellow men with guns behind every bush and our parents distraught as the local papers splashed the news:

NEWLYWEDS MURDERED ON HONEYMOON
IN MALAYA

Eventually, we managed to hitch a ride in a lorry to the nearest village, where we hired a taxi for the rest of the journey. It was not the most romantic start to our honeymoon. I never saw the car again. After our escape from the black zone we drove up to Fraser's Heights, a cool hill station where we were able to walk in the jungle and swim at the club pool. The Heights had been developed as a typical resort for the British planters and civil servants, with golf course, tennis courts, a British club (not open to Malays or Chinese), and holiday homes that would not have looked out of place in Tunbridge Wells. After a week we moved down to Port Dickson, where we had been lent a government bungalow right on the beach, with attendant Malay servants who cooked delicious Malay dishes for us.

Fraser's Heights had been a disappointment. It was quite cold and, far from needing acclimatisation, Angela much preferred the heat of the coast and we enjoyed the lovely sea bathing and the glorious sandy beaches of Port Dickson. In October 1945, the same beaches would have been the landing place for the British assault on Malaya at the end of the Second World War, but the Japanese surrender on 15 August forestalled the invasion.

The sands stretched north and south for many miles, backed by

Tony McCrum in his garden, August 2010, showing off his first book.

Robert Garmany McCrum (1829-1915), the wealthy entrepreneur and Tony's great-grandfather.

Great-grandfather's 'cottage', Milford House, Milford, Armagh, Northern Ireland.

Commander-in-Chief, *Plymouth*, Admiral Pridham-Wippell, with his personal staff, secretary, Paymaster Captain Prevett, chief of staff, Captain Leggatt and Flag Lieutenant Tony McCrum, 1947.

HMS *Duke of York*, flagship of the Commander-in-Chief, Home Fleet, 1947.

'Hands to Bathe', off the ship's side of *Duke of York* in mid-Atlantic.

Deck hockey on the quarterdeck of *Duke of York* at sea.

HMS *Implacable*, the second flagship, takes over from *Duke of York*.

HMS *Implacable* visits Oslo. The King of Norway, King Haakon, inspects the guard of honour on the flight deck, led round by Tony McCrum.

The Shaw Savill liner *Gothic*. She was converted to a royal yacht to take King George VI and Queen Elizabeth to Australia and New Zealand in 1952. The tour was aborted due to the death of the King.

First command, the destroyer HMS *Concord*, off Singapore, 1955.

The ship's company of HMS *Concord*.

Angela Long, about to become Mrs McCrum, being given away by Rear Admiral Norfolk in Singapore.

Commander and Mrs McCrum leaving the dockyard church under the traditional archway of naval swords.

Some of Tony's Chinese crew in HMS *Concord*.

NATO in Norway, 1959. The family, David, aged nearly two, and Andrew, six months, in the garden in winter in Oslo with Angela and Tony.

The farewell party in the McCrum's Oslo garden, June 1960, for the members of Tony's NATO staff – Americans, Norwegians, Danes and British – soldiers, sailors and airmen.

A final formal family photograph on leaving Norway, David in Angela's lap and Andrew in Tony's.

HMS *Meon*, headquarters ship of the Amphibious Warfare Squadron, 1961.

Some of the Amphibious Warfare Squadron in the Persian Gulf, 1961: *Meon* leading one tank landing ship, which is towing the Rhino, and three tank landing craft.

Two tank landing ships, one towing a Rhino, and one tank landing craft.

Angela with David and Andrew on the beach at Polzeath, Cornwall, in August 1961, while Tony was away in the Gulf.

The departure of Able Seaman (Bull) Brackenridge on arrival at the Seychelles after five days confined to the quarterdeck. Note his seaman's cap, which was awarded for good behaviour.

The Sultan of Socotra being greeted by his son on his return from the mainland.

The Sultan of Socotra with his luggage, accompanied by the British Resident to the Eastern Aden Protectorate.

The Captain, Amphibious Warfare Squadron, wading ashore to land at Socotra.

Meon's doctor at his makeshift surgery on Socotra. There was no doctor on the island.

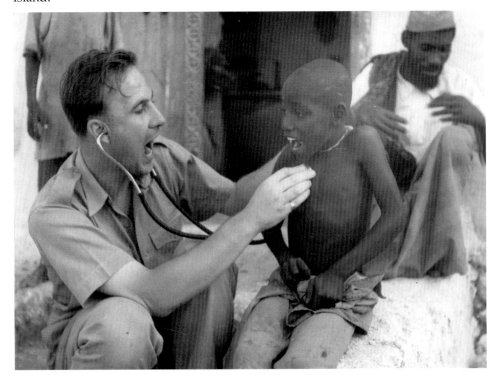

the evergreen jungle, and the coast was a 'white' zone, declared safe from the communist guerrillas. Our stay in Port Dickson was a great success but that was the end of the happy time.

Soon after we got back to Singapore, Angela developed glandular fever and was admitted to the military hospital. She had a high temperature and each time I visited her I felt absolutely miserable, leaving her looking so frail and far from home. The hospital didn't seem to know a lot about glandular fever and she was let out too soon. Glandular fever has a habit of recurring time and time again and you need to rest and do nothing strenuous for a long time to get over it. I'm an expert because three members of our family have suffered from it.

Concord's refit was coming to an end and I would have to go back to sea. With medical advice it was decided that the best plan was to get Angela home by sea and she could recuperate on the long journey back to England. We were allowed discount passages on the Royal Fleet Auxiliaries and I arranged a passage home in RFA *Bacchus*, a water carrier. It was an odd name for a water carrier; someone must have had a wry sense of humour.

After saying an anxious farewell to my sick wife, *Concord* sailed off to Hong Kong and, for the first time in my naval career, my loyalties were torn apart. I was desperately anxious about Angela, who looked so frail, but I still had my ship and her crew to worry about. So far in my naval career I had been able to concentrate entirely on my ship but now my heart and mind were thousands of miles away. It spoilt the last months of my command. Only the reassurance from an army doctor at the military hospital that no one had ever died of glandular fever kept me going. I expect I was a bit snappish with my crew but I tried hard not to let my anxieties affect my attitude towards them and I kept my worries to myself.

Soon *Concord* was on her way to the Montebello Islands, off the west coast of Australia. The islands were the site of the first British atom bomb trials. They were uninhabited except for the rats and consisted of flat, sandy scrubland – a perfect place for an atomic explosion. HMS *Plym*, an old Second World War frigate, had been impregnated with one bomb that was detonated from afar. After the explosion there was not one atom of the frigate left. Strangely, most of the rats that infested the island survived, presumably because they took refuge in their underground holes.

Concord had heard nothing of this explosion as we were far out in the Indian Ocean plotting the direction and speed of the wind to make sure the people of Western Australia did not suffer from atomic fallout. After the first test we were ordered to 'Proceed to Montebello for refuelling and to provide light-hearted relief to service personnel stationed there.' I wondered what exactly 'light-hearted' meant, but I assumed the idea was to entertain the troops holed up on Montebello. Whatever, the word 'light-hearted' stirred the imagination. When HM ships enter harbour it is normally an occasion of high ceremony. We dressed smartly; the crew paraded in serried ranks along the ship's sides and the ship was carefully squared off. As senior officers' ships were passed, the ship's company sprang smartly to attention with the pipe on the bosun's call of 'Attention', but all that jazz did not seem appropriate for an occasion of 'light-hearted relief'.

Instead, I arranged for the ship's skiffle group to serenade the anchorage from our fo'c'sle; Top of the Pops instead of Hearts of Oak. The crew were invited to get themselves into fancy dress of their own choosing, which sailors excel at given half a chance. I decided I should be the pirate chief, which seemed appropriate for a captain of one of Her Majesty's ships. The rest of the bridge crew were also dressed as pirates. I thought we had really entered into a light-hearted spirit.

The music was startling as the skiffle group rendered *When the Saints Go Marching In* and other popular songs of that era. Everyone was in high spirits and we gave the senior officer's ship three rousing cheers. So I was a trifle miffed when I made my official call on the senior officer, dressed in my best uniform with sword and medals, and he expressed some displeasure at our performance when entering harbour.

'Not upholding the best traditions of the service; inappropriate levity and so on.'

Silly old buzzard; no sense of humour, or had I let my imagination run away with me? Anyway, the sailors enjoyed it all and so did I.

During our stay we also organised sports and regattas and did our best to cheer up the existence of the shore teams. We landed and visited the area of destruction but there was nothing to see. Looking back, it was remarkably foolish to shuffle our way through the highly contaminated sand, but the dangers of the after effects of an atomic burst were not then fully known.

After a few days of trying to radiate good cheer we went off on our wind-measuring duties again, launching large hydrogen balloons and tracking them by radar and signalling back to Montebello the wind speed and direction at every thousand feet of altitude. If the upper winds were blowing towards Australia, the explosions were delayed.

We had been at sea for a week when Typhoon Wanda blew up. Typhoons always had female names in those days but in these more sensitive times both male and female names are used. We had to take avoiding action during the worst of the storm. This was a comparatively simple matter. American high altitude aircraft reported the position of the eye of the storm at regular intervals and the direction it was heading and its speed. On board, the position of the eye was plotted on the chart every half-hour, together with the likely course and the speed of its movement. The ship then made alterations of course as set out in a nautical table at stated intervals. For example, 'Alter course 20 degrees to starboard for thirty minutes; then alter course 10 degrees to port,' and so on. This system was calculated to keep the ship clear of the worst of the storm but it was still essential to use your own weather eye and experience to make sure you really were avoiding the danger. It sounds simple but it required close concentration on the reports from the aircraft as well as on following the avoidance instructions to the letter and using your common sense.

A typhoon can sink a destroyer. The Americans once lost three destroyers in a single hurricane. I was keen to avoid the same fate. I have never been interested in performing that ancient ritual where the captain of one of Her Majesty's sinking ships stands to attention on the bridge, saluting the White Ensign as the sea slowly engulfs him. Glug, glug, glug and he's gone; only his cap floating on the waves showing where he met his end.

Even though we took the right avoiding action, the wind and sea was dramatic and quite frightening and I had to be on the bridge for long hours, making sure we were correctly following the avoidance drill. In the middle of this excitement our engineer officer appeared on the bridge, ashen faced and clearly very worried.

'There is a serious leak on the stokers' mess deck, Sir. We are trying to plug it.'

I went down to the scene of the trouble and found a lot of water sloshing around the mess deck, with more coming in all the time. There was a long horizontal gash in the ship's side about a foot below the waterline and the repair parties were making heroic efforts to build an inner skin to control the leak. The danger was that the gash might extend horizontally. I thought to myself, the stokers will soon have their own swimming pool, but it wasn't really amusing. I tried to remember what the Duke of Wellington said at Waterloo when faced with a possible disaster. Sangfroid must be preserved. *Concord* had been built during the war using steel that had not been submitted to the standard quality control checks and by 1956, she was a rusty old bucket.

I went back up to the bridge to make my reports to base and turned the ship for the harbour. After reporting our leak to the shore authorities we were ordered to leave our patrol area and return to Fremantle, the port of Perth in Western Australia, and give leave. Eventually, the engineers staunched the flow of water but it was a nightmare not knowing how long the repairs would hold. We battled our way back to Fremantle at slow speed to avoid opening up the gash in the ship's side.

At Fremantle we were given a great Australian welcome and the media people came on board to interview me about our 'hurricane horror'. A slightly overheated young lady asked if I would give a talk about our experiences to the 'Women of Western Australia', which I did. I can't remember what I said, and I don't suppose it matters, and I doubt whether the audience was in double figures.

Australia is a marvellous young country and Royal Navy sailors have always found it fascinating, particularly the women. Desertion from HM ships visiting Australia has for many years been a popular pastime on the lower deck. What's more, many Australians (including the police) were quite friendly towards deserting British matelots. Indeed, had not the early settlers been minor criminals or fugitives from justice? An unhappy HM ship could lose as many as twenty or more such deserters. Every captain felt challenged to keep his score to the minimum. It would be a black mark for McCrum if my chaps took off into the bush *en masse*.

So I delivered myself of one of my more pompous addresses to the ship's company and warned them of the dangerous consequences of deserting, of the damage to the honour of the Royal Navy, Great Britain, and the Empire (we still had one then, just) and the effect on their mothers, plus any other fatuous thought that came into my head. I concluded by saying, 'Have a wonderful time, but be back on time.'

I was determined to have a wonderful time, too. I had an open invitation from an Australian family to take me on a tour of the coast down to Albany for a couple of days. After we had been in harbour a few days and the repairs were nearly complete, and we had had no problems with the sailors on leave, I felt I could take a few days' leave. We only had two serious absentees, Able Seamen Kennedy and 'Wilson' (not his real name, as he is still alive). My friends took me south down the coast road for our first night stop in Albany, a small fishing port that reminded me of some of our Cornish ports. We were hundreds of miles from the ship and duty. It was most relaxing after the recent excitements and we planned to stay the night in the local hotel and drive back the next day.

Sitting drinking in the bar, I espied a familiar figure. Surely, this was one of my two deserters, Able Seaman Kennedy. I looked again: it certainly was. What an incredible coincidence. The wretched man had fled for hundreds of miles to get safely away from the ship and from me and there was his enemy. I felt for him.

What now? There was no naval patrol to call on. I knew the local police were unlikely to arrest him. He had committed no offence in Australia. I could just see myself telling the local bobby to arrest Kennedy.

'On what charge, mate?'

'He's a deserter.'

'Are you a deserter, mate?'

'Not me, I'm just a visitor.'

'On your way, mate, I've got better things to do.'

I couldn't let things slide so I went up to Kennedy and rather feebly said, 'Hello, Kennedy, what are you doing here?' which was a really stupid question. There was no reply, not a flicker of recognition. I tried again.

'Kennedy, I know it's you … here, have the other half.'

That clinched it. We had a drink together and I managed to get him to tell me his story. Yes, he was intending to desert. His father had physically abused him repeatedly as a child and he could not face going home in six weeks time when the commission ended and he would be sent home on leave. He was still a minor, only just eighteen. For a moment I thought, why not let him go? He was a good lad and would be a hard worker and would have a great life in this young country. Let him disappear; no one would know except me. Then tradition and orthodoxy took over and I decided I had to get him back if I could. If he genuinely did not want to go home I could try and arrange for him to 'stay on station' and in the ship for the next commission. By the time he eventually went home he would be of age and his father would have no authority over him. We had the other half and he talked and talked. Eventually he said, 'I'll come back.'

I heaved a sigh of relief, but did he really mean it? There was no way I could restrain him and we were not returning until 8.00 am next morning. There was only one thing to do, trust him.

'We'll be leaving at eight outside this hotel and we'll meet then,' I said hopefully.

'Yes, Sir,' he replied, but I had my doubts.

Next morning sharp at eight o'clock there he was and I apprehended my first and only deserter. It was an awkward drive back to Fremantle with one deserter sitting in the back of the car with my host's wife, and wasn't really fair on my hosts, who had got themselves entangled in a naval mess. On arrival on board I delivered my charge to the coxswain, who was in charge of defaulters, and felt mightily relieved. Of course, he had to be punished, but I decided that he was an absentee, not a deserter. This meant a much lesser punishment, which could be carried out on board instead of in a military prison in Singapore. I was also able to arrange for him to 'remain on station' and he recommissioned the ship with the new crew and remained overseas for the next two years. He didn't try to desert again.

We were due to sail next morning and our deserter score was reasonable. So far, two men had not returned from their leave. When we came to prepare for sea early next day we were still two short. We cast off our mooring wires from the jetty and were heading for the harbour entrance when there was a shout from the inshore end of the jetty.

'Wait for me, wait for me.'

It's somewhat unusual for a naval rating to order his captain to wait for him as if he was a bus driver, but our next stop was Hong Kong. So I reversed engines and went astern alongside the jetty again. He was one of our two absentees, Leading Seaman Cundall, a very fine seaman, and I was disappointed in him. He was extremely drunk and had to be hauled on board. Then we set sail again.

Forty years later at a *Concord* reunion I heard the true story of Cundall's fall from grace. We have a reunion of the ship's company every year, when we drink and tell each other improbable stories of our time on board, usually apocryphal tales of one of my misdemeanours. Apparently, he had met three Australian girls who had taken a fancy to him. He was a handsome, husky young man of over 6 feet tall. They could not decide which of them should have him so they shared him. They more or less confined him to a hotel room, where they fed him, boozed him and enjoyed three-in-a-bed sex. Many on the lower deck thought he deserved a medal but I had to disrate him to able seaman and fine him for 'conduct to the prejudice of good order and naval discipline', a somewhat inaccurate description of a jolly romp.

Our final score of deserters was one, but not for long. 'Wilson' cleverly mingled with the crew of an Australian aircraft carrier that was also in port. One of their matelots gave him an Aussie uniform but he was soon rumbled and returned to the Royal Navy, but not to *Concord*, as we had gone by then. I think he served time in the detention quarters at Singapore.

I have never personally arrested a deserter before or since, but you never know what to expect in the Navy. I have shipped a bull from Africa to the Seychelles, nearly been knifed in a bar in Barcelona and fallen foul of an American admiral at the landing in the south of France in 1944. There is always some excitement to keep one on one's toes.

After Australia, my command was coming to an end and we went back to Hong Kong for the final weeks. Then the time came to say goodbye to our many friends. One special friend was Jenny, a friend of all on board. Jenny was our Chinese head side party girl. There was a tradition in Hong Kong that each HM ship was adopted by a 'side party' who kept the ship's side painted and washed whenever the ship was in harbour. The party usually consisted of three or four women, always women, working from a sampan, a flat bottomed boat propelled by oars and a sail, in which the women lived and worked. They also ran errands for the ship's company. Jenny ran a tight ship with three side party girls and was always waiting for us when we got into harbour. She remained loyal to *Concord* for many years through different commissions.

Years later, I was delighted to see a much older Jenny receiving an MBE from the Prince of Wales during the handover of Hong Kong to the Chinese government. She certainly deserved it, having served the Royal Navy for over fifty years, far longer than most sailors.

Other hardworking and loyal servants of the Navy were the Chinese members of our crew, the cooks, stewards and laundrymen. They performed all the service jobs and kept us clean and well served. When we got back to Hong Kong for that farewell visit I felt that they should be ceremonially thanked for their hard work and loyal service. The Chinese appreciate ceremonies and I arranged to hold a special parade for the Chinese staff on the parade ground in HMS *Tamar*, the shore base. After inspecting their ranks I made a short speech of thanks for all their hard work and for their service to the Royal Navy. Inscrutable as ever, I had no idea whether or not I had lifted their spirits.

When ships leave Hong Kong at the end of their commission all the friends of the officers and the crew come down to the jetty to wave goodbye and the naval band from the base plays sentimental tunes like *Now is the Hour*, the Maori farewell song. As we moved out of the dockyard everyone was waving, some were crying and last messages were shouted. I was too busy manoeuvring the ship out of the basin into the crowded anchorage to take it all in. Great friends for a while but never seen again; such is naval life. Many ships that pass in the night.

Command had been fascinating, sometimes burdensome, but great fun and an enormous privilege to be in charge of such an elite group of young officers, petty officers and sailors. The average age of the ship's company was only twenty-three, but I am sure if we had been put to the test of war they would have acquitted themselves with honour. We had a remarkable crew in whom I had the greatest confidence. It was an unforgettable time, without any terrible mistakes, despite one or two near misses.

Command presents many problems for a young captain. He has to live an unaccustomed lonely life on board, never becoming too familiar with any of his officers. He may like some more than others but he must not show it. He has great powers and no one on board is likely to gainsay him. It is all too easy for such power to go to his head: power corrupts. After a while you think you are always right and give short shrift to any doubters.

At sea there is the constant tension of your concern for the safety of your ship and the crew, whether from the weather, as in a typhoon, or from collision when in cluttered waters. When I was not on the bridge, I was in my sea cabin just below. Like a mother who wakes to her restless baby at night, I would wake if the officer of the watch ordered large course alterations to the helmsman and the ship's bows began to swing wildly, or if the repeated bell-like sound of the revolution counter told me he was making a big increase or decrease in speed. Should I get up and go onto the bridge to see what was happening? I usually resisted it as the officer of the watch had clear instructions as to when he should call me. I had to trust him, but sometimes it was a strain.

During training I had read books on 'leadership' but I believe they were a waste of time. There is no one classic method of leadership. It has to depend on the personality of the leader. I served under one captain who was most efficient, absolutely fair and remained aloof and very formal, but the ship's company would have followed him anywhere. Another was a very nice guy and most friendly but you never knew where you were with him. The troops had no time for him. The best, very simple advice I was given when I was a midshipman was: 'Just be yourself and always say "Good morning" with a smile to each man you pass.' That is all I tried to do.

Command is a fleeting experience and once you get ashore the glory is quickly forgotten. Many, many years later and long after I had retired from the Navy and had been left on my own by my wife's early death, I was doing my household chores. My head was down a lavatory pan giving it the weekly scrub and I suddenly burst out laughing as my mind flashed back some fifty years to my days as skipper of *Concord*. Why this odd ribaldry in a loo pan? On board *Concord*, every Saturday morning, I conducted a formal inspection of the inside of the ship – mess decks, galleys, bathrooms and the ship's heads (loos). This was an occasion of ceremony, known as Captain's Rounds, preceded by a sailor piping 'Attention' on a bosun's pipe and attended by a galaxy of officers in my wake, alert to catch every word of criticism or praise that I uttered. I would pay special attention to the ship's heads. These were cleaned by the Captain of the Heads, a long-serving able seaman who took great pride in his handiwork. Usually the result of my inspection would attract a 'Well done, Smith,' but occasionally it would be, 'Not good enough. Get right under the rim.'

What made me laugh was that now, aged eighty-six, I'm the Captain of my Heads AND the Inspecting Officer. This is my Saturday routine; head down in the pan, only it's mine, hard brush all round, bleach and scrub.

'McCrum,' I may say to myself, 'well done,' or if I am not satisfied, 'not good enough. Do it again.' This is the sort of carry on that happens if you live alone for too long at a great age. I was laughing at the irony of my situation; once I was so high and mighty but now the wheel of fate has turned full circle. What a pity Able Seaman Smith isn't there to see me.

After the farewells we sailed away to Singapore, where the changeover of ship's companies was to take place. We tied up at the same jetty where I had first walked up the gangway to take command eighteen months earlier. It was the same brief handover routine: confidential books correct and money audited.

'Have a great commission; good luck.' And I was away to the airport. I didn't look back.

I was soon on my way by air to Stanstead. We arrived on a grey overcast morning and England felt cold after the heat of Singapore. It felt even colder when I could not see Angela waiting to meet me. I had been treasuring this moment of reunion with her but I was met by her father, whom I disliked. His words of greeting were, 'Angela is in bed. She has had a relapse from her glandular fever.'

I felt bereft. We had no home of our own until we could take up my next appointment in a month's time. Her illness had gone on for six months and she was much weakened by it and we had had no married life together so far, dogged by the big G, and I had hoped that, at last, we might enjoy life together. I was utterly miserable as my father-in-law drove me to Hans Crescent in Kensington, her parents' home, and there I found a forlorn, weakened person in bed. She was even more miserable than I was. But this proved to be the final relapse and she soon recovered.

As soon as she was fit we took off for the Pembrokeshire coast and stayed with her soldier brother and walked the coastal paths. The winds of life blew through us again. It was almost a honeymoon, as the first one had been struck down by the fever. We must have suffered one of the unhappiest first years of marriage, particularly Angela.

Chapter 11

Shotley, HMS *Ganges*

Just before I left Singapore I was told where I was going next. I was thrilled to be appointed training commander and second-in-command of HMS *Ganges*, our largest boys' training school at Shotley Gate in Suffolk, just across the harbour from the port of Harwich. This suited me as I had spent much of my career training young sailors at sea, particularly young men on the lower deck who appeared to have the ability to become officers.

HMS *Ganges* was what is called a 'stone frigate', a shore-based establishment spread along the banks of a promontory between the rivers Stour and Orwell. It had been built in 1906, when the training ship HMS *Ganges*, moored in Harwich harbour, was decommissioned and all the boys moved ashore. The camp was dominated by a high mast of some 70 feet set on a windy desert of a parade ground, which formed the core of this training establishment. We had our own hospital, chapel, school and central dining hall in fine brick buildings. The living quarters consisted of long dormitories in enlarged Nissen huts. There was a large swimming pool, playing fields for every sort of sport and a yachting marina on the river. Although it didn't have some of the magnificent buildings you see at Eton the facilities were as good as those in many independent public schools. Ganges had a tremendous spirit, which seemed to be passed down from generation to generation. Many have said, 'You can always tell an ex-Ganges boy.'

The main road from Ipswich ran through Shotley village to the Harwich ferry, which transported cars and passengers across the river Stour. Across this road the newly-built officers' married quarters existed in what had been fields on the banks of the Stour. Here, all the married officers lived cheek by jowl. We had never lived in married quarters and were dubious about existing in a 'village' where all the inhabitants were naval officers. The layout had been designed so that everyone could see the maximum of each property and there was little privacy. We would have preferred to rent a house in one of the delightful Suffolk villages and get to know some of the locals. In practice, we were all very civilised and didn't gossip about each other's private lives, but we didn't much care to be surrounded by all that uniform.

The Commander's house was the last one in a row that ran along the banks of the Stour, close to the river, which was only 50 yards from our front door. There was a belt of trees along the bank with just enough depth to give a home to nightingales. When they sang for us on our first night I felt that life was good and could only get better. Soon after we arrived at Shotley, Angela told me she was definitely pregnant. The stars in the heavens seemed to shine with a radiant brilliance and I wanted to tell the whole world of this cataclysmic event. I rang my mother.

With the summer holidays over I had work to do. HMS *Ganges* trained some 1,200 young men, aged fifteen to sixteen from secondary modern schools, and a few from grammar schools. They were all volunteers and my lasting impression of them was their enthusiasm and their longing to go to sea, just as I remembered I had all those years ago at Dartmouth. They didn't have to wait as long as I did as their training was much shorter. For nearly all of them this was the first time away from home and to begin with some of them were very homesick. It was quite alien to working-class culture then to leave home at such a young age and there were a few casualties who had to go back to their parents.

The training was similar to that at Dartmouth, partly naval and technical, seamanship, boat handling and signals as well as school subjects – maths, science, and some naval history and how to write properly. Classes were smaller than in the national school system and some boys who had lagged in their secondary schools steamed ahead in the more concentrated naval educational system. The teachers also had the support of naval discipline.

Each day started with all the boys drilling on the parade ground, followed by the ceremony of 'colours', the hoisting of the White Ensign and playing of *God Save the Queen*. In the afternoons, the boys could play soccer, rugby, and hockey in the winter or take part in cricket, athletics, swimming and sailing in the summer. I spent a lot of time on the river as that had been my interest since the age of thirteen. This was a job after my own heart and one of the happiest of my naval career. I was happy in my work and happy at home.

My first captain, Michael LeFanu, had been a fantastic and unusual person to serve. He broke most of the rules of naval etiquette and procedures and got away with it. The boys loved him, although the staff were unsure about some of his antics. Staff at these establishments tended to be the most orthodox people and liked their superiors to be patterns of orthodoxy, but they loyally supported their captain, who had effectively modernised and humanised what had been a very traditional and tough outfit, rather like the Dartmouth of my day, in the thirties.

On the last night of his last term the Captain was to address the boys and the staff massed for his farewell exhortation in the huge gymnasium. I knew something was up and that he was planning a 'shocker'. I waited apprehensively on the stage with all the officers. He was late; unusual for him. At the far back entrance of the gym a late arrival boy in sailor's uniform appeared in a dishevelled state, cap awry, and uniform unpressed. He walked unsteadily down the gangway between the crowd of boys. Of course, I recognised our captain early on and realised he was putting on one of his acts for which he was famous.

As he reached the stage he turned round to face the audience and, as naval defaulters do when in front of the defaulter's table, he pulled off his cap. A shower of fags flew out. The hall erupted in glee. This was the hiding place that the boys used to stash their illicit fags. After that they listened to every word of his speech, which was serious and thoughtful. His unconventional acts always had some purpose behind them. This one was to ensure the boys and the staff listened to his advice.

The officers who came to Ganges as divisional officers

105

(housemasters) were specially selected and were a talented group of young men in their late twenties and early thirties. Assisted by chief petty officers and petty officers they took great care of their charges as well as instilling into them the purpose of naval discipline and the lores and customs of the service. One officer in particular stood out, our physical education specialist. He was a considerable sportsman and played cricket for the Navy and was in charge of athletics and swimming, where he showed great patience with struggling non-swimmers. All boys had to be able to swim before they left for sea.

One evening the telephone rang at home.

'Pat has shot himself,' reported the duty officer.

'Where?'

'In his cabin.'

'Why,' I asked.

He didn't know. I told the Captain. Shortly afterwards the police arrived and reported to the Captain. Apparently, Pat had been to the cinema in the afternoon in Ipswich and had made advances to a young man who left the cinema to complain to the police and Pat had been arrested as he left the cinema. He admitted the charge and was released pending further action. He came straight back to his cabin, took out his sporting rifle, placed the muzzle in his mouth and pulled the trigger.

In the fifties, any homosexual act was a crime with savage prison sentences for offenders. In the Navy, such people were 'dismissed from the service with disgrace'. Pat was one of the victims of what was a most inhuman law and being an honourable man had decided to spare his family and the Navy his disgrace. I was appalled at this waste of a talented and fine officer as well as a good friend.

We gave much emphasis to boatwork, both sailing and rowing, in the same type of boats that the boys would meet when they went to sea. We also had one seagoing yacht, a 50 square metre, and, amongst other qualified skippers, I sometimes took boys out into the North Sea at weekends. There is nothing like a yacht in the open sea, vulnerable to winds and currents, to teach the importance of discipline and the skill of working as a team under adverse conditions. It also gave me an informal setting to watch the boys' reactions under stress and after stress in which to try and understand the hopes and thoughts of these young men from a very different background from my own. I probably enjoyed these forays into the North Sea more than they did. I had spent many months sailing in the same sort of boats at Dartmouth and was now enjoying training the next generation.

There was one horrendous occasion when I made a classical, inexcusable, appalling error and succeeded in capsizing a whaler in Harwich harbour on a very cold autumn day. When a whaler is 'tacking', sailing into the wind, it is imperative that its keel plate should be lowered below the hull bottom to stabilise the boat from heeling too far over. We had been running before the wind. When the wind is right aft, and in this condition the keel is hoisted out of the water to increase the speed, but as soon as you alter course into the wind the keel must be lowered before the turn. I had failed to give the order and no one else remembered. Within a trice we had capsized and were swimming. We all had lifebelts on so there was no danger and the guard boat soon picked us up. But it was a disgrace for the Commander and I'm sure every instructor lapped it up with glee. 'Have you heard …?' There were also one or two snide remarks in the wardroom.

Every summer term we had a parents' day and the highlight of the day was 'manning the mast'. The mast was the centrepiece of the parade ground and nowadays it is all that is left of HMS Ganges; the mast is now a 'listed building'. The mast was spanned by two yardarms, to which in the days of sail, the mainsail and topsail would have been laced.

But on parents' day it was the focus of a fantastic tableau by some fifty boys, all volunteers. At the blast of a whistle they swarmed up the mast and spread themselves along the yardarms to a time set by the band, playing rousing sea shanties. In the midst of these boys climbing the mast one specially selected boy, called 'the button boy', could be seen climbing a rope ladder up the main stalk of the mast. On reaching the topmast he had to shin up the last few feet, hand over hand, with his legs wrapped round the top pole. He slowly hoisted himself onto the 'button' where he only had a short lightning conductor to steady himself. Then he stood erect on the button. The button was the small sphere of wood that capped the mast. It was about two feet in diameter and just wide enough to plant his feet either side of the lightning conductor, which he gripped with his knees. As he started to stand up there was a dramatic roll on the drums, which was suddenly silenced as he came to attention and saluted the parade. Every year there was an audible gasp from the onlookers, which included the boys' parents and friends. The rest of the team on the lower yardarms also stood motionless as the band struck up *Rule Britannia* and the button boy remained at the salute as frozen as a corpse.

At the blast of a whistle every boy slid rapidly down the shrouds and within seconds the mast was clear. It was a magnificent performance, heightened by the dramatic music from the band and it always drew a thunderous applause from the watchers. It never ceased to amaze me that we had so many volunteers for this hazardous event and I was mighty relieved when all the boys were safely down. I could never have done it myself.

Our new captain had joined at the beginning of the year. He had many new ideas and was a complete contrast to our previous boss. Some of us found it difficult to adjust and I look back with some dismay that I didn't support him more effectively.

This was the first time in my naval service that I had a home of my own. It was a novel experience in my life, which had completely changed, and I now had stronger attachments than the Navy, which began to recede from my life as I enjoyed the pleasures of being married and a soon-to-be father. Since I was seventeen the Navy had been first in my life and had enveloped me. Now my wife, and shortly my sons, took centre stage. To begin with I was a bit confused as to how to fit the Navy and marriage together. Sometimes I felt I wasn't devoting enough time to my efforts for Ganges and at others that I was neglecting Angela. She never complained at the long hours I had to leave her on her own. As a Wren officer she knew the strains of naval married life, the long absences, the disruption, and the abandonment when the sea claimed one for long periods.

Angela's pregnancy was nearing its climax. She had sailed through the long months, blooming more and more as the months went by. We were all set for a unique event. Just after midnight it all started – discomfort and contractions. I was convinced the baby was going to be born there and then and tried to remember what the modern husband would have to do. How does one deliver a baby? Would I have to cut the umbilical cord? The questions raced through my mind but the mother was perfectly calm. I was in a right old stew. Of course, we really had plenty of time. I rang the hospital 10 miles away in Ipswich.

'My wife's having a baby.'

'When did the contractions start?'

'An hour ago.'

'Nothing to worry about; bring her in and we'll look after her.'

On arrival at the hospital we were met by a brisk midwife. 'Shall I stay?' I asked anxiously.

'No,' said the brisk midwife. 'We'll let you know when the baby is born and when you can visit.'

I felt I had been summarily dismissed. She gave me the impression that this was women's business, in which men were merely a nuisance. I drove back to Shotley in a low mood, awash with worry, which did not last long because at 9.00 am I had to conduct the boys' full dress Sunday parade when they would march past the Captain and into church; no backsliding, all had to pray. I didn't pay much attention to our excellent padre's exhortations but prayed hard that all was going well in the maternity ward, despite the fact that I wasn't a believer.

After church on Sundays the naval custom was that the officers attended the wardroom bar before going home to their loving wives who were sweating over a hot stove to produce the typical Sunday lunch.

'Telephone call for you, Sir,' sang out the hall porter. This was it. My heart raced.

'You have a baby boy, weight 6.75lbs and in excellent health. Your wife is fine and the baby is fine. You can visit at 4.00 pm.' Alleluia!

Of course, the officers were aware of this historic event and were all hanging around to 'wet the baby's head', which meant drinks all round on the Commander. Then, as it was Sunday, a second round was called. Hugely expensive.

ABANDON SHIP!

What excitement: everybody crowded round with congratulations, probably thinking 'poor old boy having a baby at his age.' I didn't care; by this time I almost felt I had given birth myself.

After sobering up I drove to the hospital to find a tired mother after ten hours of labour and a red, wrinkly-faced infant looking like Winston Churchill in old age. It seemed a miracle and we had done it all on our own. Really Angela had 'done' nearly all of it but I felt I had played a small part.

I have to admit that I didn't immediately feel that instant rapport that I felt I should towards our firstborn son and heir. Apart from an insatiable desire to feed and sleep he didn't appear to notice people around him or show any personal characteristics.

After a couple of months I was beginning to wonder if I was an unnatural father, unmoved by this little chap who did nothing but feed, sleep and leak. Then one morning he was lying on a table after having his nappy changed and I was watching him and suddenly from nowhere came a great smile as he looked straight at me. It was a real grown-up smile of recognition. 'I know who you are and I am pleased to see you.' At that instant I fell in love with the little devil, much as one sometimes does (when young) with a beautiful girl across the room when your eyes meet and you smile at each other and the earth shakes. I realised I was normal after all and the nightingales seemed to sing every night that summer.

During our time at Shotley I had to take stock as to my future. The government wanted to reduce the size of the armed forces and redundancies were called for. If enough volunteers could be found there would be no need for any sackings. A generous redundancy package was offered and the scheme became known as the Golden Bowler Scheme.

Family life had changed my outlook and I no longer looked forward to a life on the ocean waves in exotic foreign climes without any domestic entanglements. There was a new priority in my life, accentuated by the late age at which I had married and started a family. Angela and I discussed the future and I decided to opt for a Golden Bowler and a farewell to the excitements of the sea. Applications were treated confidentially because many were refused and disappointed applicants might not want their superiors to know they had considered 'abandoning ship'. An official envelope duly appeared in my post.

> Their Lordships are unable to accept your application to resign under the provisions of the redundancy scheme.

So that was that. In many ways it was a relief. I had served my country for twenty-five years and as a commander had been reasonably successful and I greatly enjoyed the naval life. Then I made a mistake. I felt it was only right to tell my captain that I had applied and been turned down. To my dismay he thought my action bordered on treachery to the service and that I would no longer give the Navy my wholehearted loyalty. I thought he would prevent my promotion to captain but I had an important ally in the Commander-in-Chief in Chatham, who had known me in another appointment, and I heard later that he had backed me for promotion. After the disappointment of being a failed Golden Bowler it was a pleasant surprise to be the first in my Dartmouth term to be promoted to captain six months later.

During my time at Ganges, in November 1956, Anthony Eden's Conservative government committed a fatal political error when we, together with the French, invaded Egypt. The reason was that the Egyptian dictator, General Nasser, had nationalised the Suez Canal Company, which was an Anglo-French company, and seized control of the canal, which was a vital waterway on the route to the East.

When I heard of our amphibious assault and air attacks on Egyptian airfields I thought our politicians had gone mad. Servicemen and women are not expected to hold strong political views but I thought this was nonsense as it was the service personnel who were the victims of any stupid mistakes.

Only a few years earlier when we had permanently occupied the Suez Canal Zone with military forces we had found it difficult to defend and were forced to withdraw by the constant marauding attacks by Egyptian freebooters. So why, if we had not been prepared to hang on to the Canal Zone earlier, did we think we could do so now? It was crazy, uncoordinated, thinking. The politicians had not thought the matter through and had landed the three services in a humiliating retreat. Sterling was threatened and the American president, General Eisenhower, made it clear that he would not support us and this forced us to withdraw. The Suez debacle eventually forced Eden out of politics. I felt it was sad that Eden's political career should end in such a humiliating way as I remembered him as one of the few Conservatives who refused to support the appeasement of Hitler before the Second World War when he resigned his post as foreign secretary in the Chamberlain government in 1938. Now he was a broken man.

I was hostile to the whole affair and relieved that I was not taking part, but military men must do the politicians' bidding whether they agree with it or not. One can always try and resign one's commission as a protest but it is a futile action. If you sign up for the services you do whatever is required of you and keep your opinions to yourself. It's best not to have strong political views, but I always did. 'No politics, no religion, no sex,' was the convention about conversation in naval messes. What else was there to discuss? Football?

The terms flew by, the boys passed their exams and marched past the Captain for the last time and vanished off to their ships, which is what they had been longing for throughout their time at Ganges. I met several of them again at sea and I believe the Ganges training was a fine start to their naval careers.

By the beginning of the summer term of 1958 I knew my happy time at Shotley was coming to an end; two years with Angela in a normal married life and our first child. It was the first time since I was fourteen that I had had a settled family life and it had been extraordinarily happy. The job had been absorbing and rewarding watching hundreds of young lads from secondary modern schools blossoming and learning willingly. Of course there were misfits but they could leave if they wanted to. Family life had been all I hoped it would be and my next appointment to a senior NATO job in Norway meant we were going to be able to live together for another two years. Despite the joys of family life there was a twinge of regret that I would not see the sea again for another two years.

My appointment was to the staff of the Commander-in-Chief, Northern European Command, as Assistant Chief of Staff, responsible for the communications within that command. The command ran from the North Cape on the northernmost tip of Norway to Denmark and Schleswig-Holstein in Germany.

It was time to say the usual farewells and be guest of honour at dinner when impossible tributes are paid (rather like those funeral orations where the deceased appears to have been a saint whom you barely recognise). But first, summer leave, and then the journey to Norway and another fresh experience.

Chapter 12

Norway, 1958-60

We were on the move, once again. With Angela, baby and luggage stuffed into our small Cortina estate we trundled up the old Great North Road to Tynemouth to catch the Oslo ferry. Cars had to be hoisted on board by crane; there was no roll-on roll-off in those days. Then it was into a flat, calm North Sea, so unlike what I remembered from the war years when I was sweeping mines off the same coast. After a perfect North Sea crossing, what wonderful sights we shipborne travellers enjoyed as the ferry steamed up the long Oslo fjord, passing white wooden houses dotted amongst the pine trees on innumerable islands and seeing the city straight ahead under the slopes of Holmenkollen, the mountain backdrop. Only a few years earlier, Hitler's invasion fleet had steamed up the same fjord to conquer Norway.

Almost as soon as we arrived I had to leave the wretched mother, six months pregnant again, to cope on her own. This was typical of naval life but at least we were both in the same country.

I had to carry out a familiarisation tour of the command. I had two weeks to reconnoitre the Northern European Command, visit military headquarters and learn the geography. Our command was like a very long sausage, 1,300 miles starting at the Arctic Russian border and ending in Northern Germany.

Accompanied by my predecessor we took passage in a coastal ferry steamer, which went north inside the chain of islands that lie off the Norwegian coast. We stopped at every fjord to deliver or take on pigs, bullocks, hens and farm produce and it was an excellent way to understand the geography, because Norway has such a long coastline and many of the military headquarters were on the coast. The cabins were sparse and the food mostly dried fish, but luckily the places we visited laid on sumptuous meals to regale the new assistant chief of staff. In return, we presented them with bottles of duty-free whisky, which was like gold dust in Norway.

I visited radio stations, underground communications centres and military, naval and air force headquarters. Our final destination was the North Cape, a barren and desolate point whose sheer black cliffs rose out of the Arctic Sea.

As assistant chief of staff (communications) I reported to the chief of staff, a British major general, Welby-Everard, and the Commander-in-Chief was another British general, Sir Nat Murray. They were both good to work for and I much enjoyed the joint service and international atmosphere of the headquarters.

We found Norway truly delightful and the Norwegians friendly and natural. This was probably the most classless society in Europe. For many generations Norwegians had been farmers, fishermen or seamen in their large merchant fleet and the country had been ruled from Copenhagen, where the upper crust tended to live. There had been no aristocracy and no royal family until they got their independence (peacefully) in 1905, when they invited Prince Knut Olaf of Denmark to be their king and he became King Haakon of Norway. Their education system mirrored their society. There were no private schools and every child went through the same excellent state education system. Children were greatly valued and cared for. Even in those days, anyone seen smacking a child in public would have been quickly surrounded by remonstrating adults and, in our time in Norway (1958-60) , it was unheard of for a child to be abused.

At that time, Norwegian memories were still shaped by the war and they were particularly friendly towards the Brits, as we had rescued their king from the invading German army in 1940 and had liberated their country in 1945. Many of their servicemen had escaped to Scotland in fishing boats to join the Army or one of the Norwegian naval ships that had escaped the German invasion and, like Vikings of old, had carried off into marriage many a Scottish girl. So there was a great, welcoming environment for our small Anglo-Saxon family.

NORWAY 1958-60

The Northern Command Headquarters was deep under a mountain some 20 miles east of Oslo and thought to be impregnable to an atom bomb. We were in the middle of the Cold War, in an icy stage of confrontation. All the vulnerable communications systems were buried deep underground and they were my responsibility – radio, teleprinter and ciphers. These were manned by an international team of soldiers, sailors and airmen under the immediate command of a British major of the Royal Corps of Signals. The planning staff had offices in this bunker but we only used them when we carried out simulated war exercises. Otherwise we worked in office blocks outside, on the side of the mountain. We all trusted we would have enough warning of a nuclear attack to collect our papers and hurry down to our underground hidey-hole. But what about our families?

It was my first experience of managing a tri-service, international staff. The staff officers reporting directly to me were Danes, Norwegians, Americans and British and they represented all three services, navy, army and air force. It was one of the most stimulating appointments of my naval career. We were appointed as internationals and not to represent national interests, but those of NATO as a whole. Nationalities were soon forgotten in our daily work and it made little difference to me whether I was discussing a problem with an American soldier or a Norwegian sailor. My deputy was an American lieutenant colonel who found me a little difficult at times but always supported me loyally. Our internationalism sometimes angered our British officials in London if we took a decision that, to them, might seem contrary to purely British interests. This seldom happened and only occasionally caused friction. The Americans were the least international in outlook but the most loyal to their service superiors. I found it immensely encouraging working so closely and amicably with this international staff. If only nations could work together in the same way. A naïve hope.

The mission of the Northern Command was to hold a Russian invasion force advancing into northern Norway, where there was a common border. We anticipated a Russian offensive in the far, frozen Arctic, where nothing much existed except a few Laplanders and some moose. The other area we had to watch was the Baltic Sea, the

117

approaches to Denmark and North Germany, where Britain had fought the Baltic War against Russia in 1854. Our peacetime work was not arduous, mainly planning for all the possible outcomes if the Cold War suddenly became hot.

Once a year, we engaged in a full-scale 'war' exercise in the autumn, when an Anglo-American fleet and amphibious forces would steam in from the west to reinforce the small Norwegian Army and Air Force. It didn't help our war preparations that the Norwegian government would not allow NATO ground and air forces to be based on their territory in peacetime, which meant that the opening days of any conflict would be extremely dangerous for Norway and NATO. I remembered that the Nazis had destroyed the Polish Air Force in the first forty-eight hours of the Second World War and effectively eliminated all Polish resistance.

To bring in the reinforcements to Norway after the outbreak of a future war would take some time as most of the support had to come in by sea. Perhaps we would get enough warning but I doubted it. Our communications along a long, thin ribbon of Norwegian and Danish lands were extremely vulnerable to attack.

The large-scale annual land, sea and air exercise was a major test of our communications, which was central to the success of the exercise. After all the effort to work up the systems to wartime perfection it sometimes flitted through my mind that it would be fascinating to see how all our plans would work in practice, but the horrors of a nuclear war quickly extinguished such imaginings. I hoped we were keeping the peace and that our wartime preparations would never be needed. I had read much European history and I concluded that Russia was more often the attacked than the attacker.

Would the Soviets have launched a war of aggression in 1958? I doubted it. They had fewer nuclear weapons than the Americans but far more troops on the ground. Any sign of weakness where a country already had a strong communist presence might be tested and, if the cement was crumbly, the walls would be attacked using the local communists, as they had done in Czechoslovakia. I wondered sometimes if there was more danger from an American miscalculation, or an erroneous warning signal from the early warning system might start a nuclear conflagration. On balance, I concluded that my wife and family were safe in Norway and I did not expect World War III.

Our family life in Oslo could only be described as idyllic. Our son David was developing rapidly and it was fascinating to watch him as he developed from babyhood into childhood. Sometimes, however, the shadow of the past hovered over me as I remembered the death of my brother as a small child in Hong Kong in 1922, and I felt if it happened again in our generation to one of our sons I would have found it very difficult to bear. I appreciated for the first time the agony of my parents all those years ago.

To our delight, Number Two was due in September 1958, only three months after we arrived in Norway. We settled into Norwegian life, living amongst the local population and making friends with our neighbours. We tried in vain to learn Norwegian but as everyone wanted to speak English we soon gave up. Before the snows came we had the excitement of bringing into the world our Norwegian-born baby. He caused us a bit of a problem as he turned up a bit earlier than expected. We were finishing a rather up-market dinner party. The British Ambassador had left and the other guests then departed. One of the lady guests lived alone in our street and I escorted her home. On my return, panic struck. Angela was lying on the sofa with her legs crossed.

'My waters have broken.'

Fifteen months earlier I had been panic stricken when Number One was on his way. Now I thought I was a more mature father, but this was panic stations again. I rang the Red Cross clinic where Angela was booked in. It was only ten minutes away and I bundled her into the car. We arrived at the clinic to find the building in total darkness, not a chink of light anywhere, all doors locked.

'Keep your legs crossed,' I cried. It was all I could think of. Perhaps I meant 'fingers crossed'.

I called out, 'Hallo, hallo, is anyone there?'

There was no response. Then I remembered stories of young swains trying to attract the attention of their lovers by throwing stones up at their windows. I picked up some gravel from the drive and flung it at a window where a light had come on. The window opened and a face poked out.

'The baby is coming soon,' I yelled.

'OK, OK, soon be down.'

In Norway, fathers nearly always attended the birth and I stood by rather helplessly. The Norwegians are a hardy race and the midwife was a matter-of-fact lady, who seemed impervious to the cries of the mother.

'What about gas and air?' I asked as I could not stand the pain any longer.

'She not hurting,' was the response.

At that, my well brought-up wife who had never been known to utter so much as a 'damn' burst forth with, 'She bloody well is; it's bloody painful,' whereupon, I was shown how to operate the gas and air machine.

All went well and, within the hour, our 'Norwegian' baby, Andrew, or Andreas, as the Norwegians called him, was born. We had only just made it but what a wonderful experience to see the entry of a new life into the world.

I suppose most parents feel that a safe birth and new life is a miracle. I certainly did and it had been a rewarding experience to be with Angela during the birth. We were both very excited and I stayed until morning, when I still had to go to the headquarters. Paternity leave? What's that?

One of the most beautiful seasons in Norway is the spring, late May, when the snows have melted and the sides of the fjords are covered in cascades of white and pink fruit blossom flowing down the mountainsides, with the snow still lying on the tops of the mountains. In the spring of 1959 we drove over the mountain plateau and across to the western fjords, staying in small hotels on the water's edge. Later in the summer, we drove east to Sweden for a visit to Stockholm. I had last visited Stockholm as a 17-year-old cadet in the naval training cruiser HMS *Frobisher*, and my friend John and I had had a frustrating time visiting the family of a professor from Uppsala University. We had been invited to lunch to meet his two beautiful daughters and we had expected to be shown round Stockholm by the two lovelies. Instead, we were taken to the opera, where we had to listen to a fat lady singing in German. We were sitting in a very hot box, in which both of us disgraced the Royal Navy by falling asleep. We were never left alone with the girls. What a reputation British sailors must have had.

In the summers we could be down on the beach of our nearest fjord within twenty minutes and laze in the hot sunshine. Norway has a brief summer, June, July and early August. It may be short but it is usually fine, warm and sunny and it was wonderful to watch our two sons getting used to sand and water.

Soon it was 1960, and we were coming to the end of our time of great happiness. We had been together as a close family for two years. Angela and I had had a normal married life, which was unusual for those in the Navy. I think we had made the most of it.

Our time in Norway had flown by. It was June 1960, and there were the inevitable sad farewells and presentations. On the last day, a crowd of friends came down to the boat to see us off and we sailed down the fjord waving till the figures disappeared. It was a perfect way to leave, with a two-day cruise across the North Sea to Tynemouth, far better than the modern trail out to an unfriendly airport and a cramped journey with squalling infants and frustrated passengers.

By now I knew I was going to the Persian Gulf to command the Amphibious Warfare Squadron, and would be away from the family for thirteen months. A sad separation but an interesting job.

Chapter 13

Amphibious Warfare Squadron
Nov 1960–Feb 1962

W hat next? The appointment read, 'Captain Amphibious Warfare Squadron and in command HMS *Meon*'. This was a lovely job in the wrong place, Aden (now Yemen), a barren and extremely hot location at the bottom of the Red Sea. I wondered if I had committed some awful gaffe as it was a common belief in naval circles that 'difficult' officers were appointed to ships in the Persian Gulf and Red Sea areas to let them stew in the heat and get them out of the way. I did have four wartime Mediterranean D-Day landings under my belt so it could have been that Their Lordships of the Admiralty thought that that experience would come in handy.

HMS *Meon* was an ex–Second World War anti-submarine frigate that had seen service in the Battle of the Atlantic and had been converted to act as a headquarters ship for a brigade-sized assault landing, a smaller version of the headquarters ships I had served on at the Sicily, Salerno, Anzio and South of France landings. It was familiar territory.

The rest of the squadron consisted of two tank landing ships (LST), four tank landing craft (LCT) and a Rhino, not an animal but an invaluable, shallow draft, motorised pontoon that could trundle to and from ships to the landing beach when the water was too shallow for the landing ships to beach. Then the tanks could roll out of the landing ships onto the Rhino and be deposited ashore. An LST was a ship, not unlike a medium-sized cross channel car ferry, with bow doors that opened to allow the tanks to roll out onto the beach. Each LST could carry half a squadron (six) of tanks and it also carried infantry assault craft (LCA) hoisted on davits either side of the ship. These LCAs could be loaded with infantry or equipment, or both. They were shallow draught and could normally run right up onto the beach. The LCTs were much smaller than the LSTs and similar to a cross river car ferry. Each LCT could carry two tanks, a number of armoured cars or a piece of artillery.

Before I could be allowed to take charge of this arsenal, Their Lordships of the Admiralty had to be assured that McCrum still knew how to go to sea. I had been ashore since 1956, over four years. My hull was a bit rusty. First we had a long leave when we got back from Norway and we had to find a house because my appointment was what was called 'unaccompanied'. This simply meant that the Admiralty wouldn't pay for any family travel or accommodation abroad. In any case, family life in the Gulf in those days would have been impossible. There was no suitable accommodation, few non-Arab local families, and it was extremely hot in the days before air conditioning. We couldn't have afforded the travel and accommodation in a hotel and never seriously considered it. We felt it was better for the family to remain settled in England.

Angela and I were both used to these naval absences but for me this was the most painful of all. I had had four gloriously happy years close to my wife and watching our little boys grow and develop, crawling, walking, talking, even being ill, and had enjoyed every minute of it. Now I would not see them again for thirteen months and would miss those fascinating years of development in small children between the ages of two and five. As so often happens in the Navy, there was the tug of war between the joys of being at sea in a fascinating job and the sadness of absence from those most dear to me.

My refresher courses took place in Portsmouth, conveniently close to home, and I was also sent on an update on the latest thinking on amphibious operations in Devon, but they were still stuck in the timeframe of Second World War assaults. Nothing much had changed from my experiences in the four Mediterranean landings.

AMPHIBIOUS WARFARE SQUADRON

A few weeks before Christmas, the time came to say goodbye, the first time that I had left my family for more than a day or two. Would the children even recognise me when I came back?

After heartrending farewells and floods of tears, some of them mine, I was off to Stanstead Airport on a cold, grey, miserable November early morning. To me, the whole world seemed grey. Two days later, we landed at Khormaksar airfield in Aden, in the searing heat of the Arabian desert. Met by my predecessor, I went straight onboard my flagship, HMS *Meon*, not as svelte and beautiful as *Concord*, but command of a ship is always exciting. I was beginning to shake off the blues.

What would I make of it? Would my family concerns affect my performance? This was the first time I had had a command and a wife and young family back home to think about. I had the routine command responsibilities for the welfare and safety of my crew and my ship but this time I had the rest of the squadron to watch and guide. Apart from my own ship, I was responsible for the effectiveness of the squadron as an assault weapon and this was my prime concern. We were a small cell of amphibious capability remaining from the huge armadas that landed on D-Day in Normandy. Would we be called upon again?

A novelty of this command was that we kept half a squadron (six) of tanks and their crews and their impedimenta permanently embarked in an LST so that we could intervene swiftly to meet any threat. The Army crews were rotated every three months to avoid them getting too bored. I felt it was most important to do everything possible to uphold the morale of these floating soldiers.

My predecessor, John Lloyd, and I counted the money, checked the ciphers, had a farewell tot and that was all there was to handing over the Amphibious Warfare Squadron. My immediate concern was to assess the state of my own ship and her ship's company and to get up to speed with the contingency plans for assault landings in the Middle East.

Walking round your own ship and talking to petty officers and sailors is always a pleasure and gives you a feel for the state of morale and of the standard of cleanliness and seamanship of the vessel. I quickly concluded that much needed to be done to bring *Meon* up to scratch. The crew looked sloppy and there seemed to be rather a casual approach to discipline. I decided to replace my first lieutenant but it took some time for the Admiralty to find a new one and we had an uncomfortable few weeks.

My second and probably more important task was to study the secret contingency plans that set out the threats to British interests in East Africa, the Red Sea and the Persian Gulf. We had two firm treaty commitments in the area. The first was to support Jordan if attacked and the second was to defend Kuwait, which was still under British colonial rule. Iraq had a longstanding claim to Kuwait as it had been one of its provinces in the time of the Ottoman Empire, ruled from Constantinople. The Ottoman Empire, pre-1914, ruled over a swathe of the Middle East from Kurdistan and Iraq in the east to the Red Sea in the west. It included Syria, Lebanon and Palestine. The Ottoman Empire had been dismantled by the victorious Allies at the end of the First World War when we defeated the Turks, who fought on the side of the Germans. Iraq, Kuwait and Palestine became British Protectorates and Syria and Lebanon went to the French.

The more closely I studied the plans the more I became convinced that the Amphibious Warfare Squadron (AWS) was based in the wrong place. It was typical of some idea of political comprise between the two plans. The squadron was 1,400 miles from Jordan and 2,100 miles from Kuwait. It was an ageing outfit with a poor turn of speed. It would take us six days to reach Aqaba in Jordan at the top of the Red Sea and nine days to reach Kuwait in the Gulf if we had the wind behind us. I did not really believe Britain would go to war on behalf of Jordan if it was attacked by Israel, the most likely aggressor, and it was most unlikely that an adjacent Arab country, Saudi Arabia, would attack it. If Israel had attacked Jordan it would probably have been supported by the US, which had a long and close attachment to Israel. Would Britain then have supported Jordan? I doubted it, particularly after our experience at Suez.

I concluded that the Jordanian threat ought to be put on the back burner and that Kuwait was a much more realistic target for an Iraqi invasion, with at least some legitimacy behind it. Iraqi tanks could threaten Kuwait within a few days. It seemed obvious to me that the AWS should be based at Bahrain, an excellent British base in the Persian Gulf, within two days' sailing of Kuwait. After thinking long and hard I wrote to my admiral in Bahrain, the steeplechasing Roy Talbot, who was in charge of naval operations in the Middle East, as Flag Officer, Middle East. I set out my proposals for moving the AWS and all its stores and beach landing equipment to the Gulf. He swiftly approved.

It was also important for me to learn *Meon's* capabilities as a seagoing vessel and I took her to sea for a day of manoeuvres and exercises. Every ship has her own idiosyncrasies and it is important for a captain to learn how to handle her well. Manoeuvring with skill at sea and in harbour, particularly in harbour where spectators abound and the naval ones are always ready to pick holes in the performance, is a vital test. So when a new captain joins his ship he likes to show off his ship-handling skills – above all, a smart 'come alongside' the jetty on return from sea, a dashing but accurate approach and then the order, 'Stop both engines,' followed by, 'Half-speed astern,' to reduce the speed of the vessel and a final 'Stop both engines,' and she should be parked in the correct slot alongside the jetty, or that is what he hopes for. The fewer movements of the ship's engines there are, the more skilful the manoeuvre.

I had mastered my last ship, a fast greyhound, and I was now ready to show my new officers how it should be done. After our first day at sea we were returning to harbour in Aden. The jetty was just off the main street and quite easy to approach. Jetty ahead, approach angle just right and a spanking speed. Now I'll show them how to do it with panache. Nearly there …

'Stop both engines. Half-speed astern.'

Not much reaction; the ship sailed on.

'Full-speed astern,' (supposed only to be used in emergencies). But on we went. On and on. Slowly we ground to a halt, almost 100 yards beyond the jetty. Oh! Colossal mortification. Officers on the bridge looking down their noses and trying not to grin. I was devastated.

I had hopelessly misjudged the difference in the astern power of a frigate's engines compared to a destroyer's. I should have taken my first 'come alongside' with much more care. There flashed through my mind the words of the officer of the watch in HMS *Royal Oak* twenty-five years earlier when I was a young midshipman driving a picket boat: 'Far too fast McCrum: go round again,' and that is what I had to do now. Right round in a large circle and a fresh approach. The next day I took *Meon* to sea again and punished myself with endless ship handling manoeuvres until I was near perfect.

As soon as the arrangements for our move were complete we set off for the Gulf, *Meon* leading the squadron at a stately speed of 10 knots. We trundled along the south Arabian coast and reached the mountainous coastline of Oman, where the mountains were so close to the shore they seemed to rise up out of the sea. At the end of the coast of Oman we turned sharp left into the Straits of Hormuz, only 25 miles across between Iran and Oman. It is an important choke point at the entrance to the Gulf and easy for Iran to close it and seriously disrupt oil supplies from the Gulf.

The Gulf is like a long finger pointing north-west out of the Indian Ocean. It is excessively hot in the summer with temperatures of 45-50°C in the open, enclosed by the Saudi desert on the western side and the Iranian desert on the eastern side. The winters are pleasantly cool from late November to early March, when it begins to hot-up. In 1960, ships had very limited air conditioning. In *Meon*, the only conditioning was in the operations room and my day cabin, and even there, the temperature in the middle of the day made desk work almost impossible; the brain simply seized-up and refused to operate. The heat on the mess decks was appalling. In the boiler and engine rooms down below we had to keep a very close watch out for sudden heat exhaustion.

The problem of heat was a constant danger, of which we all had to be aware. It strikes suddenly and without much warning and if a man began to suffer from heat exhaustion he had to be given first aid at once. He would be placed in a cold bath with as much ice as could be found and his temperature taken frequently so that he could be whipped out of the bath before his temperature fell too low. Heat also caused behavioural problems; men behaved irrationally and tempers were short. Minor disciplinary spats easily got out of hand. It was vital for ships' captains to keep a close watch on the morale of their ships' companies and a listening ear for any grievances.

There was one problem that the Navy swept under the carpet. I know of no research, literature or guidance on the subject of celibacy amongst seagoing officers and ratings, deprived of their wives' and girlfriends' affections for many months, even years. How did Nelson's crews satisfy their sexual urges when they were away from home for nearly three years? It was a worry for us in the Gulf. There was some anecdotal evidence that hot climates enhanced sexual appetites and desires and I could vouch for this personally. In *Meon* I had some 100, mostly young men, shut up in a steel box, cheek by jowl. There was none of the usual civilised shore life they were used to: no pubs, except the naval canteen, no brothels, no families. This greatly concerned me, not that I could do much about it.

At that time, while the homophobic laws of the early twentieth century were not being pursued so vigorously in civilian society, the Navy was unremitting in its pursuit of deviant behaviour. I was dismayed, but not particularly surprised, when the First Lieutenant warned me that he had received a complaint by an 18-year-old ordinary seaman of sexual abuse by a senior rating.

'Who is he accusing?' I asked.

'I'm afraid it's Chief Petty Officer 'Smith', Sir.'

I was appalled. I knew Smith well. He was the senior chief petty officer in charge of all seamen working on the upper deck, the chief boatswain's mate. He had proved himself to be a fine seaman and an excellent man manager. He was married and had an unblemished service record going back many years and was not far off retirement and pension. I also liked the man; he was loyal and hardworking.

This was a court-martial offence and I dreaded having to deal with it. In such serious cases there has first to be a court of enquiry to establish the prima facie evidence. This proved conclusively that the abuse had occurred, only abuse on the lesser scale, sometimes called 'touching up'. It was not a case of buggery. The rule in such cases is that the captain of the ship has to be the prosecuting authority. There is no let-out and I dreaded it.

We managed to find a British lawyer in Bahrain to defend the accused and I hoped he would produce a vigorous defence. The court martial was convened in the naval base. The court consisted of three officers, of whom the senior, a captain, was president. There was also a judge advocate (clerk of the court), a qualified naval officer lawyer to advise the court on the law.

I said my piece and called my witnesses. The defence lawyer cross-examined them but failed to shake them. I thought he made a poor fist of it.

Verdict: Guilty.

A plea in mitigation was made by the defence. I was so dismayed by the weakness of the defence's plea that I took the unusual step of asking the president if I could add to the plea in mitigation. Being a naval officer I think he too felt the accused had not had a good deal from his lawyer and he allowed me to speak. I told the court that Smith was a first-class chief petty officer and a person I respected and that this offence was completely out of character. I reminded the court of the conditions in a ship in the Gulf, the intolerable heat on board, the lack of civilised amenities ashore and his deprivation of normal marital and family life, but my eloquence was wasted. The sentence was severe: dismissal from the service with disgrace.

This meant he would be put on the next available plane home and on arrival, his uniform would be taken off him and a civilian suit issued instead and a railway warrant issued to his home address. His pay was stopped at the moment he was found guilty and he would be on the dole. He would also lose his pension rights. It was a terribly harsh sentence and I went back on board my ship and felt ashamed of myself and ashamed of the Navy and of our society. It was another six years before these homophobic laws were repealed when Parliament passed the Sexual Offences Act 1967.

We were lucky in having a fine group of captains in all the ships but I was particularly concerned for the soldiers embarked for three months with their tanks and who didn't have too much to do except when we landed for exercises. In my own ship I spent time wandering around talking to the sailors, some of whom I remembered having been trained by me in HMS *Ganges*. This helped me to understand how they were reacting to the difficult conditions on board.

AMPHIBIOUS WARFARE SQUADRON

Since about 1820, the Persian Gulf States along the western shores of the Persian Gulf and the Gulf of Oman had been the concern of British governments, and the waters off their coasts, of the Royal Navy. This interest started when the East India Company in India began to trade with Mesopotamia and Persia. At that time, the largely arid Gulf States were more interested in piracy and slave trading than trade. The Royal Navy, in support of British trade, suppressed the slave trade and the piracy and established the British government as the protectors of the independence of the states. In other words, we took them over.

At this time, in 1960, all the small Gulf States along the eastern coast from Oman to Kuwait were under British control. The Gulf was a British lake and nothing moved without our say-so. Oil had not been discovered, except in Bahrain and Kuwait, and life in Abu Dhabi, Dubai, Qatar, Sharjah and Oman was still primitive. The internal governments of each of these states were left largely in the hands of the local Arab rulers with a British Resident domiciled in each country to see fair play. Britain took responsibility for defence and foreign affairs. There was a high commissioner in Bahrain to guide the affairs of the Gulf States and to oversee the Residents.

The Gulf States were one of the few remaining outposts of British Empire. India, Pakistan, Burma and Ceylon had all been granted independence in 1947. In 1948 we had handed Palestine over to the UN. Between 1957, when Ghana was the first African colony to be granted independence, and 1960, most of the African colonies became independent. Our Arabian dependencies, Aden, the Eastern Aden Protectorates and the Gulf States and Hong Kong, and a scattering of islands all over the globe, were amongst the last relics of Empire.

From time to time, I was required to call on the sheikhs of these states to show the flag and reinforce the mystique of Empire, rapidly vanishing. This was an occasion of ceremony, wearing full dress white uniform with medals and sword. Disembarking on a rickety jetty I would be driven in an equally rickety Jeep to the sheikh's 'castle'. This was a large, round mud and brick structure, with a bare earth floor, and was pleasantly cool.

ABANDON SHIP!

The sheikh greeted me at the entrance, just a wide slit in the wall. When my eyes became accustomed to the gloom I could see a circle of his retainers sitting cross-legged on the floor cradling their rifles. I trusted they were friendly. A huge bowl of teeming rice was placed between the sheikh and me and I was doing my best to sit cross-legged on the floor without my sword getting entangled between my thighs and doing the family jewels permanent harm. At all costs I must avoid pitching headfirst into the steaming rice. I wondered if this was going to be the notorious sheep's eyes dinner, where for the sake of Britain, one was required to pop a few fried sheep's eyes down the gullet. No, the rice concealed only goat or lamb chunks.

The sheikh and I had no common language and I watched carefully to see how he tackled the meal. No implements were provided. He collected pieces of meat in his fingers, braced his head back and popped it all in. I did my best to follow his technique. Then, as a special mark of esteem and appreciation of my visit, he fished a special titbit of meat and offered it in his fingers. I had been warned about this and it had to be accepted with great gusto as it was a mark of honour – not just one piece, but several. Should one give a massive belch of appreciation? I decided not. The things one does for one's country. At least it wasn't sheep's eyes, and one was not expected to linger.

The call was returned the next day, and the sheikh was brought off in my barge and received with a seven-gun salute and a guard of honour with fixed bayonets on the quarterdeck. He shook hands with all the officers and I escorted him to my cabin for refreshments – orange juice and small eats. An aide whispered that the boss also enjoyed a nip of whisky in the orange juice, which was strictly forbidden by Mohammed. I felt this let me off the teetotal hook and I downed a large gin and tonic. Such a ceremonial visit was typical throughout the British protectorates in the Gulf. A few years later, oil was discovered and their lives were transformed.

The role of the Navy in the Gulf was to protect the rather fragile, small Gulf States from a possible takeover by either Saudi Arabia, their mighty neighbour to the west, or from Iran on the eastern shores. Looming in the far north was Iraq, with its sights on Kuwait. Our job

132

was to keep the peace and that was the *raison d'être* of maintaining an assault capability in the area, to protect the Gulf States from possible aggression.

The Saudis had made one minor excursion into our area when they occupied the disputed country around the Buraimi Oasis; they had eventually backed off under pressure from the UK, but by far the most likely threat to peace was the Iraqi claim to Kuwait. The Royal Navy also kept a wary eye on possible outbreaks of piracy. Our presence in the Gulf may have been out of kilter with the times when the old idea of empires had died but we did keep the peace throughout the Arabian Seas and in the Gulf. There was no piracy and no war.

One of the more extraordinary outposts of Empire was the oil town of Abadan in Iran, not even a British dependency. It was owned by the Anglo-Iranian Oil Company, now BP, and it was run as if it was a suburban Surrey town and completely controlled by the company. It must have been a major irritant to the Iranian government who had suffered from a long history of British interference in their affairs. Jointly with the Soviet Union we had invaded Iran during the Second World War when we feared the German armies in the Caucasus might break through into Iran and cut off our oil supplies. In 1953, we had helped to oust the nationalist premier, Mossadeq, who had nationalised the oil fields. It is not surprising that in the twenty-first century Iranian governments have no great love for Britain.

One of our tasks in the Gulf was, occasionally, to show the flag in Abadan. For Christmas 1961 we were chosen (ordered) to spend the festive season in Abadan and entertain the oil wallahs. Abadan, on the banks of the river Euphrates, was an extraordinary colonial outpost in a foreign land. Well regimented trees had been made to flower in the middle of the desert to line the roads, creating leafy avenues. There were neat semi-detached houses for the lower orders, fine detached dwellings for the managers and baronial mansions for the top dogs. It all looked totally inappropriate for a desert town in Iran.

What exotic pleasures awaited us? When I told the ship's company of our Christmas plans I tried to make it sound as exciting as possible but they weren't fooled. In return for inviting lots of expat oil men on board for duty-free booze, they would ask us back for Christmas dinner.

We arrived on Christmas Eve. *Meon* and two tank landing craft tied up alongside a smelly oil-loading jetty in a tight little bunch.

On Christmas Day, I took a truncated Christmas service on our quarterdeck – a few carols and prayers, but definitely no sermon. Then I set out on the Navy's Christmas ritual to traipse round the mess decks where the crew live and radiate good cheer and demonstrate that their captain was human after all. A tot of rum was provided in each mess and a 'Merry Christmas' was toasted. This was called 'sippers' and if you were wise, it was all you would drink of each tot. There were five mess decks to visit plus a final lethal call on the home of the chief and petty officers. I survived by judiciously sipping slowly and leaving at least half a glass behind a locker in each mess. I kept reminding myself that I still had to run this drinks marathon in each of the two landing craft and then sit down to Christmas dinner in our wardroom.

I staggered round the two landing craft and Christmas grew merrier and merrier, but I remained upright and managed my dinner at 2.30 pm, by which time it was a truly splendiferous celebration. After a few hours' rest it was then off to another Christmas dinner with a charming oil boss and his wife. Who says we don't earn our pay? But I would much rather have been playing Father Christmas with my young family at home.

I didn't spend much time worrying about the political set-up in the Gulf and the decline of Empire, much my most important concern was the maintenance of the sailor's morale in this hellhole. There was virtually no civilised life for the sailors to enjoy ashore. Most men stayed on board. There was some sport when it wasn't too hot – football, hockey, cricket and tennis – but it was limited. The Persian Gulf in recent years had seen mutiny in HM ships, the ultimate horror and disgrace for a captain.

I believed that the best counter to the heat and boredom was to work hard. As soon as we arrived at Bahrain I took the squadron up and down the Gulf, exercising landing operations under every sort of beach and tidal conditions. We beached the landing ships and craft and disembarked the tanks; we unloaded the beach roadways; we set up the beach signal stations and all the paraphernalia of an assault landing. We tested ourselves to the limit. To gauge the efficiency of each ship I took passage in each one in turn and watched their assault procedures and summed up their captains. This was great for me but perhaps less so for the skippers to have their boss breathing down their necks. Gradually we became an effective assault force.

After daytime exercises we sometimes organised large-scale picnics on the beaches in the cool of the evening and landed as many sailors and soldiers as was prudent. A huge bonfire would be lit and beer was allowed and there was always someone who had an accordion to lead the singsong when we had all had enough to eat. It was the nearest we could get to a good time in the Gulf.

One solo relaxation I allowed myself was a walk in the desert. After an exercise was over and the gear was being reloaded I enjoyed taking off into the wide open desert sands, much as I used to in the lonely hills of Dartmoor. The popular conception of desert is of a flat, desolate ochre-coloured wasteland. Actually, the landscape is far more varied, with high mountains and deep chasms in Sinai and Oman and many other places. Off the western shores of the Gulf the terrain was undulating with small hills enclosing dry wadis (small valleys), with good, firm walking. With a setting sun, the reflected colours from the hills and valleys were stunning, throwing out every colour in the spectrum as the sun slowly sank over the hills and the shadows crept along the valleys. As far as the eye could see there was no sign of civilisation; not a road or car, not a house or town, not a human being, not a sound, just the mighty isolation of an empty land. It was wonderfully restorative, but I couldn't go far as time was short.

I was still convinced that the only real threat in the Gulf was from an Iraqi invasion of Kuwait, so I tried to lay plans for a successful landing, whether it was opposed or not. The key to such plans was to locate beaches where tanks could be landed safely and the exits from the beach were suitable for their deployment. This meant careful beach reconnaissance as we had done in the Second World War. This was denied to us, even though Kuwait was our ally. The British resident in

Kuwait, after taking soundings from the Kuwaiti royal family, decided it might incite the Iraqis and refused permission for any beach reconnaissance. We therefore lacked that vital piece of information needed for a successful landing. It very nearly thwarted our attempts to support Kuwait when it was threatened by Iraq in the following year.

In February 1961, we sailed to Mombasa in Kenya for a brief docking session. Afterwards and as a reward for our hard work in the Gulf we were allowed a recreational visit to the Seychelles, then an island far out in the Indian Ocean accessible only from the sea. As we were about to sail I received a signal from the Admiralty.

> To The Captain, Amphibious Warfare Squadron,
> HMS *Meon*. Important.
> You are to embark one pedigree bull in Mombasa
> and transport it with utmost care to the Seychelles.

An extract from the *Mombasa Times* of 14 February 1961 reads:

> The Governor of the Seychelles sent an SOS to the
> Admiralty in London for assistance in getting
> Brackenbridge Francise, a 500 pound bull, to the
> islands as all civilian ships have refused to take him
> and there is at present no bull on the island and the
> cows are wilting.

It was hardly the sort of important assault mission that the flagship of a squadron of six assault ships was trained for, a mere bull carrier. What a come-down. But the Navy is always full of surprises. 'Not ours to reason why.'

We soon rallied and I issued the following Order of the Day to the ship's company:

> As there is at present no satisfactory bull in the
> Seychelles and as there are 200 unmarried cows
> eagerly awaiting his arrival, I am sure the ship's

company will appreciate this is one of the most important missions ever performed by *Meon*. On no account must the bull be fed with titbits, nor does it like being goofed at. Able Seaman Robinson is hereby rated Honorary Specialist Qualification Bull Keeper 2nd Class (Unpaid).

Robinson had grown up on a Devon farm and had tended bulls from childhood.

'Lovely creatures, if properly handled, Sir.'

'I'll take your word for it. Good luck,' I replied.

Now where could we put the beast? *Meon* had originally been designed as an anti-submarine frigate for the war in the Atlantic. A small ship couldn't possibly stow a bull down below. It would never get through the hatchways. He couldn't go up in the bows of the ship or he might be swept overboard in rough seas. Black mark for McCrum. The only possible place was right aft on the sacred quarterdeck, which was only about 25 feet long and 15 feet wide, and open to the sea and sky. The petty officer in charge of the quarterdeck would have to be handled with care. The idea of a rampant bull messing up his spanking clean deck would not thrill him. I put it to him as a challenge.

'Aye, aye, Sir, if you say so,' he grumpily accepted.

The great day of embarkation came and the bull, accompanied by a government vet, arrived on the jetty, butting and kicking, definitely displeased. Two slings were passed under his belly and hooked onto the crane and he was hoisted on high. One loudly bellowing bull was thus transferred to one of Her Majesty's ships, which he promptly defaced with his natural functions. A great start.

After four days at sea we arrived in the Seychelles. The unpaid bull keeper had him completely under control all the way. For the bull's good conduct on voyage he was awarded the honorary rank of Able Seaman (Bull) and he wore an able seaman's cap with pride as he went ashore. We were all quite sad to see him go, especially the bull keeper.

The Admiralty briefing notes on the islands warned us that the population was an interesting mixture of the offspring of French,

Arab, Indian and British seamen and that the women were renowned for their sexual friskiness and disease. Apparently, there were not enough men to go round and anyway, the girls liked lots of it. Our sailors were warned of the dangers of sexual encounters but I knew that it would make not a blind bit of difference and that the doctor would be busy on the return journey. I berthed the ship alongside a wooden jetty connected to the shore by a long pontoon, at the far end of which could be seen a selection of the local beauty waiting to pounce.

I was put up ashore by the Governor in an elegant colonial residence and was given a wonderful time being shown the island and its perfect beaches. It was a welcome change from the heat of the Gulf, but we were soon on our way back there and to our first visit to Mina Al Ahmedi, the Kuwaiti oil terminal for tankers, a foul-smelling port. While we were there I was driven across the desert for a useful briefing on the political situation with the British Resident. It also gave me a chance to assess the terrain for our tanks. Kuwait Town lies on a promontory of flat desert surrounded by sea on its northern and eastern sides. On the west it is wide open to the desert, as flat as a pancake for miles around, and excellent tank country. Its only possible line of defence is a long ridge of sand about 100 feet high on the northern border with Iraq, the Al Mutla Ridge.

Chapter 14

Operation Vantage

At this time, 1961, the Iraqi dictator was General Kassem, who had led an army coup to depose the pro-British King Faisal in 1958. The revolutionaries had invaded the palace and herded the royal family outside, ordered them to face the walls of the palace and shot them, including some of the women. Kassem was a minor thug, not on the grand scale of Iraq's last dictator, Saddam Hussein, who, in his turn, had Kassem executed in 1963 when he took over.

If we had to go to the aid of Kuwait to forestall an Iraqi incursion our one hope was to get our tanks ashore in Kuwait as quickly as possible and to fly in the infantry and air support. It would be a race against time. We had a sizeable garrison in Aden and RAF airfields at Bahrain and Sharjah in the Gulf. A commando ship carrying a Royal Marine commando brigade was sometimes on station in the Indian Ocean. Then there was my squadron, with six tanks embarked and a further six tanks carried in the War Department LST *Empire Gull* stationed at Bahrain, but their crews were in Aden and would have to be flown in. There were also some stockpiled tanks in Kuwait, but they would also have to await the arrival of their crews by air.

It was all a bit of a hotchpotch and heavily dependent on air transport. If we could get our six tanks ashore rapidly we hoped this would warn Kassem that we meant business and that we would defend Kuwait. There were also the three frigates of the Persian Gulf Squadron who would act as a bombardment and anti-submarine force. We had no minesweepers. Our military forces were slender but the contingency plan had been well laid and the operation would be controlled by the Commander-in-Chief in Aden, Air Marshal Sir Charles Elworthy, for whom I had a great respect.

On 19 June 1961, Britain granted full independence to Kuwait. This apparently caused Kassem to think we might be losing interest in Kuwait, so on 25 June, he issued an Extraordinary Decree appointing the Emir of Kuwait as Qaimaqam of Kuwait in the province of Basra. The title made him a mere provincial governor and effectively incorporated Kuwait as a province of Iraq without asking the Kuwaitis if they minded. Neither the Kuwaitis nor the British paid a blind bit of notice to this blatant attempt at a takeover. Now what would Kassem do next? This was a warning shot.

By 28 June alarm bells were ringing. My squadron, consisting of *Meon*, the LST *Striker* and the LCTs *Parapet*, *Bastion* and *Redoubt*, was ordered to be ready to sail to Kuwait at thirty minutes' notice. The military attaché in Baghdad signalled that a complete tank regiment would be in Basra on the morning of 1 July and would be within striking distance of Kuwait.

At noon on 29 June, *Meon* and *Striker*, towing the Rhino, were ordered to sail for Kuwait and patrol off the coast, but to keep out of sight of land so as not to alert the Iraqis. We had to wait for the Emir of Kuwait to formally request British assistance before we could land our armour. I was greatly relieved to be on our way as we were a slow-moving outfit and I wanted to be sure to get the tanks and other armour ashore before any Iraqi tanks reached the border. It looked as if the reason we were in the Gulf was about to be tested.

On the way north I ordered ships to 'Prepare for War'. This is an order to ships to get everything ready on board in case we were attacked by sea or from the air. We connected fire hoses, ammunitioned the guns, set up first aid posts and damage control positions and many other measures to ensure top fighting efficiency. It also served to 'pep up' the ships' companies and bring them to full alert. Most of our sailors had not seen war service.

Our biggest problem was where to land the tanks. Despite our requests, the Emir of Kuwait had still refused to allow us to carry out any beach reconnaissance, which is vital to the success of an amphibious operation. Are there any rocks that might tear out the bottom of tank landing ships? Is the beach surface firm enough to stand the weight of the tanks? What exits are there for the heavy vehicles to clear rapidly off the beach? What are the gradients of the sea bed offshore? Without this information we were blind. On a previous visit to Mina, the oil port of Kuwait, I had organised bathing parties on a number of the more likely beaches and we did our best to take soundings and examine the beaches for their suitability. The only outcome of this illegal bathing activity was that none of the bathing beaches were suitable. I suppose that was a help, but not much.

On the next day, 30 June, intelligence told us that an Iraqi attack was imminent. It looked as if we were going to war. At 4.00 pm, *Meon* and *Striker* arrived in the waiting position close to Kuwait to await further orders. We were now ready to go in. A full-scale *shemal* (desert sandstorm) blew up – a thick, yellow fog peppered with sand that sticks in your throat and covers everything with a fine yellow dust. Visibility was down to less than a mile.

At midnight, the Emir of Kuwait formally requested the military assistance of the British Government and this gave us the go-ahead to implement Operation Vantage, the plan for all naval, military and air force units to come to the aid of the Kuwaitis. 'D'-day was next day, 1 July, and 'H'-hour, the time for landing the tanks, was 1100. There was not much time to find a beach and land our armour in less than twelve hours. We steamed at full speed for the coast.

There was only one possible beach near Kuwait and I sent our beach recce team ashore for a quick look. After an hour they reported it was a no go. It was now 0900, only two hours to 'H'-hour.

I scrapped the idea of landing the armour over the beaches and asked permission from my admiral to enter the commercial port of Kuwait, where there might be a slipway that could take the Rhino, and we steamed at full speed for Shuwaikh, the port of Kuwait, 25 miles away. I must admit, the adrenalin was really flowing and we were all strung up, not quite knowing what to expect. War is beastly but it is also exhilarating and I hadn't felt so galvanised since the end of the Second World War.

To lighten our spirits, the *shemal* also lifted and the sun came out. As we entered Kuwaiti national waters, I ordered *Meon* to go to Action

Stations and prepare for possible air attack. It is always better to be prepared for the worst than be caught with your trousers down. We really didn't know what to expect. Were we at war? What was the enemy threat? We donned our steel helmets and extremely hot anti-flash gear to protect us from the heat of explosions. We manned the few guns we had and were prepared for all comers. It felt ridiculous, the more so as we entered the bay and were amazed to see the local population disporting themselves with the usual weekend sports – sailing, picnicking and water skiing – swooping around us in speed boats with the passengers waving and shouting a welcome. We waved back but we must have looked like aliens in our anti-flash helmets and gloves and our faces enclosed in gas masks. There were we all togged up in our war paint, sweating profusely in the heat, but of the enemy there was no sign. It was surreal. We soon reverted to normal.

I had sent a signal to the British political agent asking him to arrange for the port director to meet me on arrival and, after anchoring, I went ashore to find out where we could land the tanks. There was no one to meet me and worse was to follow. When I tried to walk to the port director's office, some extraordinarily zealous Kuwaiti Home Guards refused to let me move and threatened to arrest me. They said they were expecting a parachute landing and no one was to move in the port area. Furthermore, they told me that the port workers were on strike as a protest against the threatened Iraqi invasion. The port was deserted: no cranes, no berthing parties, no help for us who were trying to come to their aid. What more did we need for a perfect 100 per cent cock-up?

I was in despair. 'H'-hour had passed and we were no nearer landing the armour. Then, at our blackest hour, came a saviour, an ex-chief petty officer RN who was a member of the construction company that was developing the port. Did we want to land some tanks, he asked. You bet.

I told him we had been prevented by the port guards from moving to a slipway shown on the chart and asked if he could help. Then there was more bad news. He told me that the slipway had been demolished as part of the port extensions, but he thought there might be a hardstanding about a mile further upriver. First we would have to get passes, so we piled into his car and drove like fury and got passes and an Arab interpreter. We raced back to the port and picked up the beach recce team and, at last, at 1345 hours we reached a concrete hardstanding that might be suitable, but the approaches still had to be checked for water depths. The checks showed there wasn't enough water to take *Striker*, which meant that the unloading of the tanks would have to be by Rhino, which is extremely slow. To add to the merriment of the day, the *shemal* had worsened and the visibility in the swirling sandstorm was only 1,000 yards.

We needed to get *Striker* as close to the hard as possible to cut down the Rhino's slow passage time. I was most anxious for *Striker's* safety in the appalling weather conditions and her captain not knowing exactly where the hard was. I commandeered a tug and managed to get on board *Striker* to show her captain where to go. She had to sail up a long narrow channel and carry out the tricky operation of putting three anchors down to hold her fast against wind and tide.

By 1600 hours, we were at last ready to ferry the tanks ashore by the Rhino. We speeded up the old rhinoceros by strapping four assault craft, two each side, to give her extra boost. She was an awesome sight as she forged to and fro at a speed for which she had not been designed. By 1720 hours, the first tanks were ashore. It had been a nightmare day but at last we were on the way. All six tanks were landed by 1855 hours and the tireless Rhino was drafted to land the heavy equipment for 42 Royal Marine Commando, which had arrived in HMS *Bulwark*. This involved a 12-mile round trip to *Bulwark*, anchored at the entrance to the bay. The Rhino worked on tirelessly throughout the night.

By this time, the whole of 42 RM Commando had been landed from *Bulwark* by 'chopper' at the airfield. The earlier attempt to land two companies directly onto the Al Mutla Ridge was thwarted by elements of the Kuwaiti Army, who had unexpectedly taken up positions on the ridge. In their enthusiasm it was considered likely that they would open fire on any airborne force landing troops there, whether they were friendly or not. Two companies of the Coldstream Guards, flown in from Bahrain, had also landed at the airfield, and a squadron of RAF fighters from Shahjah had arrived to protect it. Would this be enough to stop Kassem?

143

By the evening of 'D'-day, after a fairly chaotic twenty-four hours, there were substantial military forces on the ground and our tanks had reached the Al Mutla Ridge, our defensive position. This display of force apparently made Kassem realise we would fight and the Iraqi tanks advanced no further.

Once the tanks were ashore I went back on board my headquarters ship, anchored off the port, and had to deal with a number of signals from Prime Minister Harold Macmillan, who wanted to know, 'How many tanks are ashore?' and later, 'When will all the tanks have landed?'

Politicians interfering in operations are a nightmare. My own bosses weren't worrying me with details. To keep the PM quiet I anticipated slightly and replied that six tanks were already ashore and all twelve would be landed shortly. Actually, the remaining six tanks in *Empire Gull* were not due to be landed until the next day, 2 July, when the invaluable Rhino would be available after unloading *Bulwark*.

At 0700 hours on 2 July, I took *Meon* alongside the jetty in the commercial port and she became the Naval Movements and Communications Centre and, for the first time in forty-eight hours, I was able to have a breather and take stock. It had been a frantic two days but we did succeed in preventing the invasion of Kuwait. *Meon's* main role now was to be the communications hub for Operation Vantage and we handled a heavy volume of signals traffic for all three services and for the Ministry of Defence. Our work was much appreciated by the Commander-in-Chief, who wrote in his report that HMS *Meon* played a key role in the maintenance of communications and that 'the ageing ships and craft of the Royal Navy's only Amphibious Warfare Squadron had played an important part in Operation Vantage.' It was a pleasing compliment for all our ships' companies.

Due to the speed with which the operation was mounted there was no naval public relations team and I was instructed by my boss to be the naval spokesman. Had I ever received any training for this? No; I hadn't a clue what to do. We set up a daily briefing for the newspapers and radio correspondents and I tried to answer all their questions as honestly as I could. If they looked like getting too close to secret or very sensitive news I found they could usually be diverted by a 'human interest' story. They were much more interested in the heroic efforts of Leading Seaman Smith of Glasgow driving the Rhino throughout the night while his wife was having his first child at home. It was useful experience and I enjoyed the new challenge.

There weren't many light-hearted moments in this operation, but one sticks in my mind. To give *Meon's* crew some light relief we organised a beach quoits championship on the jetty just as I had played on the sands of North Cornwall. We marked out a court and rigged up a net, found some rubber rings and had some keen games. One afternoon when I was playing for the wardroom team a fleet of limousines drew up and out stepped the Emir and his entourage to watch the extraordinary capering of those peculiar British. I halted play to pay my respects and explained who I was. He thanked me for all we had done and watched the play for a while and then drove off. I wondered what he thought of it all.

By midday on 3 July the landing craft and ships of the AW Squadron had completed unloading all their vehicles and equipment and sailed individually back to Bahrain. *Meon* remained in harbour until the operation was wound down. I reported to the Commander-in-Chief that, 'One of the most satisfying features of Operation Vantage was the remarkable response of all officers and ratings of the Amphibious Warfare Squadron and the War Department landing ships who worked very long hours under most trying conditions.' We had had to use the ships' companies of *Meon* and others to unload the heavy equipment carried in the LCTs as the port workers were still on strike. This was really hot 'coolie' labour at all hours of the day and night and it caused the only serious disciplinary problem in the whole of the operation, and was certainly brought on by the heat.

Two young seamen from my ship refused to obey the orders of a petty officer. At this time we were 'on active service', when it is vital that lawful orders are obeyed without question. These two young men were working below decks under terribly hot conditions, but orders must be obeyed. The usual naval procedure in such cases was followed. The duty officer was informed. He explained to the offenders the seriousness of their offence and told them they would have a second chance to obey the order and the petty officer then gave the order again and again they refused to comply. Next day, the offenders were brought before me at the defaulters' table and I listened to the case for the prosecution and the defence by the men's representative. It was an open and shut case and I decided they had to be made an example of. Disobedience in an HM ship is extremely dangerous to morale. If people get away with it, it can spread like a forest fire, a short step then to mass unrest and mutiny. I 'stood the case over,' a naval term for a pause to consider the case and the scale of punishment. I decided that the seriousness of the offence while on active service justified a heavy sentence; ninety days' detention in the military prison in Aden. It was important to send a clear message to the crew.

A few weeks later I received an ominous Admiralty letter asking for my written reasons for the sentence and a full description of the offence and a copy of the defence statement. There had been a parliamentary question from the men's MP, instigated by their parents. Every captain dreads PQs, as they are called, as one becomes involved in party politics, which the Navy tries to steer clear of. The gentlemen in Whitehall do not always understand the complexities and threats in ships on active service and if the captain is deemed to be in the wrong it is a big black mark on his history sheet. I was worried.

In due course the Admiralty reply arrived: 'No further action will be taken in the case of Ordinary Seamen .... Your decision is approved.'

Phew! Much relief.

It had certainly been an unorthodox landing, hardly up to Second World War standards, but it had been exciting and satisfying to be doing what we had been training for all those hot and dreary months in the Gulf.

Why had we succeeded in stopping Kassem?

Our forces were close by. We didn't have to consult the UN and wait for resolutions to be passed. We had no allies to consult. Our commander-in-chief reacted with speed and gave clear and concise orders and all the units involved were well trained.

Not a single life was lost on either side. Compare this with the first Gulf War, when Saddam Hussein invaded Kuwait and inflicted terrible cruelties on the people of Kuwait. Over 100,000 soldiers from America, Britain, France and Saudi Arabia had to be concentrated near the Iraqi border and, after endless discussions in the UN, we went to war and threw the Iraqis out of Kuwait. The Iraqi Army was heavily defeated and it suffered huge casualties when the Americans mass bombed their retreating forces as they fled across the desert to Basra.

More recently, the second Gulf War has caused enormous casualties amongst the Iraqis and this time the Americans and we have had a number of killed and wounded.

Isn't preventing a war far better than a fighting war?

Chapter 15

Absence Makes the Heart Grow Fonder

fter the excitements and stresses of Operation Vantage, a period of calm caused me to reflect on the problems of command on active service. During the operation I had the responsibility for the operational effectiveness of the squadron and also for the command of my own ship, *Meon*. It was a wide remit, worrying about Able Seaman Smith's morale and welfare on the one hand, to controlling a somewhat chaotic amphibious landing on the other. I had excellent ship's officers to help me run *Meon* and I could leave much of the detailed daily routine to them. I also had a small amphibious staff to assist in the control of the squadron's operations. It was headed by a major, Royal Marines, who was extremely experienced and performed with exemplary efficiency. I was well supported.

Whatever strategic concerns I might have had about our land support for the Kuwaitis, the safety of my ship and her crew remained my prime concern. I had a young and willing crew who put up with appalling conditions on the lower deck with the usual grim, naval humour.

The dual responsibilities of ship command and squadron oversight did not worry me. By this time in my career, aged forty-two, with three years' service as a captain, I was self-confident and assured in my naval experience and I felt on top of my job.

While the excitement of live operations did assuage the

unhappiness of absence from my family I still found it sad to be away from my wife and family for such a long time. I was never much good at letter writing so I tried audio tapes instead to keep in touch with them. In a rather futile attempt to communicate with my two sons I used to sing them some nursery rhymes. Whenever I wrote a letter home I included a tape of my rendering of a rhyme sung in a rather toneless tenor. I never could sing a note, but I fondly imagined my two sons listening agog to Dad crooning away and feeling he was still around.

One morning I was sitting at my desk trying to look industrious while singing a nursery rhyme, *Baa Baa Black Sheep, Have you any wool* .... I was always very careful that no one should listen in to these nursery occasions. After all, I was supposed to be The Great White Warrior Chief, ready to lead his squadron into action against the enemy. On this particular morning I got carried away by my performance and did not notice a young signalman waiting just inside the door to show me my signals. The look of astonishment on his face said it all. 'The skipper's gone round the twist with the heat and all.' What a tale he would have to regale in the mess decks.

'Just singing to my boys,' I explained. Better if I'd kept silent.

Service in the Indian Ocean and the Arabian Seas is often unusual. A few weeks after the invasion scare had been dealt with, *Meon* was ordered to go off on her own and leave the landing ships behind. It was assumed that the Iraqi threat was dead in the water for a long time.

We were required to go to Makhalla, the capital of the Eastern Aden Protectorate, and collect the British Resident and the Sultan of Socotra and take the latter back to his island. On the way to Makhalla, we were to carry out the annual medical visit to Masirah Island off the coast of Oman, one of many possessions left over from the days of Empire. The little island appeared to be completely barren. There were a few nomadic goatherds tending scraggy sheep and some goats on a most inhospitable terrain. There were no villages and no civilisation. The population was living in the same way as they must have done in Old Testament times, in caves and Bedu tents. Once a year, a British ship visited to inspect the health of the inhabitants and

150

provide medical support. We would evacuate anyone seriously ill to the mainland.

I landed with an interpreter and our doctor, who had a booklet of advice on local customs. Sick women would not show any part of their body to any man (except their husbands, I presume), nor would they describe any sensitive parts such as their breasts. Our interpreter translated and he knew that when a woman pointed to her right foot it meant the pain was in her right breast. How did she differentiate when the pain really was in her right foot? The medical examinations were somewhat long and drawn-out, but there weren't many takers. The women were too frightened.

With our doctor I walked the width of the island to see this amazing relic of ancient history. We saw no water and it was difficult to see how they scratched a living. A few years later it was turned into an RAF airfield and the inhabitants were evacuated to the mainland. I hope they were more comfortable.

From Masirah we steamed along the south coast of Oman, a rocky hill region with purple mountains striding like giants along the coastline with, occasionally, a small huddle of whitewashed houses perched on the shore. This was where our SAS fought a long and unpublicised struggle with Omani rebels, backed by the Soviet Union, and where, after hard fighting, they won the struggle.

It was a fascinating trip, following the coastline closely and ending up in Makhalla. This was an unspoiled medieval Arab city, which had been left undisturbed under the ruler, a sultan. The British Resident represented the colonial power but it was a very light hand on the tiller.

The ancient city was beautiful in a chaotic, noisome way with narrow streets cutting through soaring balconied terraces above small courts with lemon and orange trees growing in their middle. We had arrived at Makhalla in response to a signal from the Commander-in-Chief in Aden.

> To *Meon*. Proceed to Makhalla; embark Resident Commissioner, Eastern Aden Protectorates and the Sultan of Socotra and his retinue and land them on Socotra.

ABANDON SHIP!

The Sultan of Socotra was going home after a visit to his overlord on the mainland. Socotra is an island some 220 miles off the North African Somali coast. By some accident of the colonial carve-up, Socotra came under the jurisdiction of the Aden Protectorate, although it was closer to Africa. We had never imposed direct colonial rule but it was within our sphere of interest, hence the presence of the Resident. It was a lovely, unspoilt island paradise, dotted with jungle-clad mountains, never too hot, being in the middle of the Indian Ocean. There were no internal combustion engines and no motorised transport. Clay mud huts lined the sand-surfaced streets of the minute capital. The houses, though primitive, had a simple beauty of design. The first thing that hit me when I landed was the amazing silence, broken only by children calling out as they played. No buzz of machines; no traffic noise, just peace and quiet. This idyll was shattered at the end of Empire when Aden came under Soviet influence and the Russians turned it into a huge military and naval base.

This was an important occasion as the sultan was returning to his sultanate after his visit to the mainland. Full ceremonial was called for with the Resident Commissioner in attendance. My instructions were clear. The dignity and position of the sultan was paramount, as was that of the representative of Empire, the Resident Commissioner. I knew my place, a mere naval captain, commanding the Amphibious Warfare Squadron. The difficulty was that Socotra had no port, no jetty and no landing places, just an open, shingly beach facing the long swells of the Indian Ocean. Not an easy place for a landing of high ceremony. My ship, HMS *Meon*, had to anchor well offshore.

The sultan, a neat little man in long Arab white costume and skull cap, and the rather overweight commissioner in his full white colonial uniform with medals and sword, and I in my best naval tropical white uniform with sword and medals, were almost enough to sink our small motor boat, let alone run it up on to the beach. We chugged towards the shore, where a crowd of loyal Socotrans, including the sultan's young sons, awaited us. As I feared, the motor boat grounded some way offshore. How was I to get Their Eminences onto the beach dry shod in all their finery and with their dignity intact?

ABSENCE MAKES THE HEART GROW FONDER

The irreverent part of me thought, 'Why don't they just wade ashore? It's only waist-deep.' No, my instructions were clear. This was an important ceremonial occasion and the dignity of the two principals was paramount. The best I could do was to order our beefy 6-foot bowman into the sea and instruct him to put the sultan on his shoulders and tuck his little feet under his armpits and deposit him dry-shod on the beach. The commissioner, rather a pompous man and very conscious of his Imperial position, was not a wader. So another sailor had to cart him ashore and only just made it. I wickedly hoped he might fall off and make a lovely splash in the sea.

What about me? Not quite as pompous as the commissioner but I was part of the ceremonial. Unfortunately, after mounting the two principals onto their steeds, the boat slewed broadside onto the wind and sea and began taking in water. There was only the coxswain left on board. There was only one thing for it: McCrum would have to go over the side and keep the bows into wind. I had to forget my self-importance and become a member of the boat's crew. Off came sword, medals and jacket and, clad only in my long white trousers, I performed my crew duties and got extremely wet.

Eventually, we followed St Paul's advice and cast out some sort of lash-up anchor and I waded ashore *en deshabille*, quite displeased. By the time I got ashore the sultan's welcome home was over and he and the commissioner had already departed for some sort of powwow to which I was not invited.

I had much more fun. Children appeared, curious, in the sandy street and shyly produced a football. The boat's crew and I had a hilarious kick about in and out of the little mud-baked houses, the Royal Navy vs the Socotra Scouts.

In due course the commissioner appeared and resumed his throne on the bowman's shoulders and we got him back aboard dry-shod while a rather damp captain, Amphibious Warfare Squadron, struggled into his wet Number One uniform for a formal return to the headquarters ship.

I shared my cabin with the commissioner all the way back to Makhalla and entertained him with my duty-free spirits, with which, being at sea, I could not participate. We never really connected. I suppose he had the weight of Empire on his shoulders. We landed him at Makhalla and I never heard another word from him. Not even a thank you card.

After depositing the Resident, *Meon* had to return to Mombasa for her annual refit and I flew back to Bahrain to supervise the rest of the AW Squadron. I was sorry to leave my ship behind but I had a competent first lieutenant and he would be delighted to get rid of me and assume temporary command.

I then lived ashore in the naval base and set up the offices of the AW Squadron nearby. I didn't like being ashore so I disturbed the commanding officers of the LSTs and LCTs by going to sea with them and observing their performance and inspecting their crews. Using one of the landing ships as my temporary headquarters, we continued exercising assault landing techniques, including night operations, but we were not called upon again for any more live operations.

This time ashore gave me the space to think seriously about my future. Until I married, the Navy had always had the first call on me. Whatever the Navy wanted me to do, I did it without second thoughts. If the Navy had wanted me to go and climb the North Pole, I would have had a go. Now life had changed and there was a more important focus on my wife and my children. They came first.

For a long time I had been thinking about early retirement. I now had a wife and family whom I longed to live with all the time, not just occasionally between sea appointments. I had missed them dreadfully during this time in the Gulf, but retiring was a huge step. I had reached a senior position in the Navy and was on what was called the 'fast track' for promotion. There was an even chance, no more, of becoming an admiral. The Navy had been my home for nearly thirty years and all the experience that I had gained in those years would be lost and I would have to start learning all over again in a strange civilian world. The Navy gives you a wonderfully varied experience when you are single, but it becomes an emotional tug of war after you marry. I loved the sea and the relationships with ships' companies and that satisfying feeling of being totally self-confident in my profession. I let my thoughts simmer, to be discussed when I got home.

ABSENCE MAKES THE HEART GROW FONDER

As Christmas approached, the second Christmas away from home and family, a bombshell landed on my desk – a letter from the Admiralty offering me a plum job in the Admiralty as Assistant Director of Naval Plans. This was a prestigious appointment. I knew the director under whom I would serve, Captain Frewen, an old friend from my days in *Duke of York*, but there was a sharp sting in the tail of the last paragraph. I would be required to stay in the Gulf for a further five months – a total of eighteen months away from home and family.

It is an awful strain on a marriage to separate husband and wife for so long and I was counting the days until I went home.

I was beginning to wilt under the Gulf heat and the strain of maintaining the morale of the ships of the squadron under these conditions and our readiness to defend Kuwait against any more Iraqi incursions. Senior command is lonely and you can't go around offloading your family worries and concerns about your own life onto your officers. You must always appear calm and assured even when you are boiling emotionally inside.

I chewed over the Admiralty letter for many days and it forced me to make a decision, subject to discussing it with Angela when I got home. I would retire and this meant I must refuse this interesting appointment. The job would have been an interesting Whitehall experience but it would not be fair to the Navy or my future boss if, after a few months in the job, I told him, 'I'm off.'

But the absolute deciding factor was that I could not face staying any longer in the Gulf, being an absentee husband and father. I wrote a feeble letter refusing the appointment, saying that pen-pushing wasn't my style and I did not think I would be suitable for the job. This wasn't really true, but I didn't want to commit myself finally to asking to retire until I had talked it over with Angela and had been home for some weeks away from the artificial atmosphere of the Gulf. My refusal of the job was accepted.

February soon came and *Meon* was on her way back from her refit. It was time to say the goodbyes. My petty officers and chief petty officers invited me for a farewell drink at their club in the naval base and I knew what that meant. On these occasions their aim was to get their captain horizontal and I was well aware of this and determined not to fall. After a pleasant evening and a few pints I took a taxi back to my sleeping quarters (I was still ashore). As I got out of the taxi my legs disappeared: gone, nothing below the waist. My mind was quite clear and I knew at once what had happened. They had spiked my beer. Vodka or gin in beer is virtually undetectable and the result is a knockout drop.

I was determined that no one should have the satisfaction of observing the captain of the Amphibious Warfare Squadron in this state. Nearby there was a roundabout that was covered in a thicket of shrubs on the main road into the naval base. I crawled slowly into the middle of the bushes, well hidden from spying eyes, and stretched out. It was strange that I felt completely sober, no nausea, no dizziness, and my mind was crystal-clear. There I lay, occasionally testing my legs for vertical strength. After an hour or so the strength in my legs began to return and soon I was upright and I walked back to my cabin to sleep for the rest of the night.

A few days later I was packed and ready to go home. Thirteen long months of absence had finally come to an end. What would I find at home? Would the children remember me? David had been three and Andrew two when I had left. Long naval absences share one problem; the wife has been running the show while the husband has been away, coping with the children and such things as paying the bills and finding a plumber. When the man returns he can feel shut out of family life and the wife may not want to release those responsibilities. The children defer to the mother and may see their father as a stranger who has no rights over them. The readjustment requires much tact and love. I knew the problems. How would I cope?

In late afternoon I left *Meon* anchored in the bay off the naval base. She was probably going to be my last command and also my last seagoing ship. It was my farewell to the sea. It's always sad leaving a ship; each one takes on a life of its own and leaves its mark on you. They had all been different: *Frobisher*, *Royal Oak*, *Basilisk*, *Skipjack*, *Bridlington*, *Mendip*, *Largs*, *Biscayne*, *Tartar*, *Duke of York*, *Implacable*, *Concord* and *Meon*, the last of the line. They had each given me a home for parts of my life, in peace and war.

ABSENCE MAKES THE HEART GROW FONDER

There is a sentence in the *Naval Form of Prayer to be Used at Sea* where we prayed for: 'Such as pass on the seas on their lawful occasions.'

For the past twenty-five years I had been a small part of the Royal Navy, whose main peacetime task was to protect and assist those 'who passed on the seas on their lawful occasions.' Now I was leaving my last ship and, as the motor boat carrying me and my luggage ashore for the flight home left the ship's side, it suddenly hit me. This was the end of my life at sea; the completion of my seagoing mission. I realised I was throwing away all those years of training, of knowledge of the sea and its winds and storms, of aspects of human nature revealed in sailors under conditions of peril and disaffection – a huge naval seagoing experience that was never to be called on again. I had also climbed the greasy pole of success and I felt I was at the peak of my powers.

As the boat chugged across the harbour I was surprised to see a lone figure on the bridge waving a towel in farewell and below him on deck, groups of sailors saluted me with three cheers: 'thank gawd he's gone.' I looked again at that lone figure and recognised him as a petty officer who had come to me a few days earlier in some personal anguish. We had had a long talk and I had been able to give him some comfort. I waved back at him to give him reassurance but it was me who needed the reassurance. I was throwing away all my seagoing experience and knowledge and embarking on a journey that would take me into an unknown civilian world.

As my ship receded into the haze of the desert heat it became smaller and smaller and the curtain came down on my seagoing career. I nearly wept.

I was quickly brought back to sanity when I checked in at the entrance to Bahrain Airport and prepared for the tedious business of departures. I was surprised to be met by the airport commandant, who escorted me to the terminal building. This had never happened before and nor has it since. He ushered me to the VIP lounge to a private room where he had laid on a surprise dinner party with my squadron commanding officers and a few local friends. The usual tedious check-in formalities were waived; instead I enjoyed an excellent meal. To my dismay all the passengers were embarked first and then I was escorted by the commandant to the aircraft, much to the annoyance of the other passengers who had been kept waiting. It was altogether an unexpected and heartening send-off from the Gulf and my seagoing career.

As we rose over the harbour the small dot that was *Meon* shone in the evening sun and I pondered on what we had achieved in the last thirteen months. The ship's company had been reasonably content, despite the heat. The out-of–date Second World War ships of the AW Squadron had become an effective assault force of limited potential, able to intervene in crises. When put to the test we had performed and achieved what we were supposed to have done. We had kept the peace in the Gulf.

After an overnight stop in Nicosia we arrived at Heathrow at midday the next day. There is a well-known Victorian painting called *The Sailor's Return*, which depicts a Royal Navy able seaman arriving at his Portsmouth home after a long absence at sea, being greeted by his devoted wife standing in the doorway with arms outstretched. Behind her stands a gaggle of children smiling and welcoming him home.

This twentieth century sailor arrived home by air to be welcomed by his wife at the exit in a Heathrow terminal, having been through baggage recovery and customs. Despite the grisly arrival routine I was longing for our reunion. I looked in vain for the smiling face. All I could see were hordes of chauffeurs holding up placards showing the names of people they expected to meet … Heywood-Barker, Ahmed Khan, Smith …. Where was that happy little face with its shy grin?

The much longed-for reunion with Angela was thwarted by a series of mishaps. She, misinformed, was at one terminal and I had arrived at another. Attempts to locate each other failed. Mislaid in Heathrow is an experience that provokes bad temper, particularly when it's your wife who has been mislaid.

After my thirteen months in the Gulf I was home, but the arrival at Heathrow had been a disaster, frustrating and deeply disappointing. In my imagination I had pictured such a happy meeting and a swift drive home by car to see the children in Petersfield in Hampshire. Now I would have to get home by public transport – Tube to London; another Tube to Waterloo to catch the next train to Petersfield and finally a taxi home. I felt miserable.

ABSENCE MAKES THE HEART GROW FONDER

Hours later than expected, I reached home alone. I opened the front door. In our cottage the stairs swept straight up ahead from the door. Sitting quietly at the top of the stairs, David, our elder son, was waiting for us. Would he remember me? It had been a long time and he had only been three when I left.

Then, a beautiful, welcoming smile spread across his face and my heart jumped with joy, all woes forgotten. I rushed up the stairs and took him in my arms and hugged and hugged him. I would never go to sea again.

Angela returned soon after, having had a terribly frustrating time at Heathrow, and we were all reunited. This was one of life's golden moments and it made me even more certain that I wanted to leave the service.

Chapter 16

Sunset

Six wonderful weeks of Foreign Service leave and reintegration with the family followed, during which I was appointed Vice-President of the Admiralty Interview Board, which sat in HMS *Sultan*, a naval engineering school near Gosport, close to my childhood home in Alverstoke. It was quite nostalgic.

All the aspiring schoolboys who wanted to become naval officers were interviewed here. The 16-year-olds were destined for the Royal Naval College at Dartmouth and a full naval career. Eighteen and 21-year-olds were candidates for short service commissions, many of them for the Fleet Air Arm. The board was presided over by a rear admiral and the other members were a grammar or public school headmaster, a junior naval officer, myself, a senior Admiralty civil servant, who was the head office spy to make sure we tried hard to find some good working class candidates, and a psychologist who revealed the inner secrets of the teenage mind.

We were a diverse crew but we had one common aim: to find candidates who would meet the demands of the naval service and who would enjoy the life. We saw a huge array of talents and met with some extraordinary responses to that ordinary question, 'Why do you want to join the Navy?' including one lad who said that he wasn't sure, but his father was very keen.

The day of inquisition started at 8.00 am in the gym, where the candidates were split into groups and given physical tasks to perform, such as building a bridge across an imaginary chasm. This was followed by classroom sessions where they were given problems to assess their individual reasoning capabilities.

ABANDON SHIP!

'You represent a town council planning committee. The town badly needs a large new car park to encourage the inhabitants of the surrounding villages to shop in town. Cost £2,000,000. The town also desperately needs low cost housing on the same site, which is the only one available for housing. Cost £10,000,000. Which proposal should the committee back? Discuss and decide and report your findings to the board'.

We sat back and watched the interaction of the candidates as they discussed the problem. We weren't particularly interested in their solution but in their reactions to one another and their clarity of thought. Some of these conundrums brought to the fore the quieter, less bossy, boys who may not have done well in the physical tasks. During the day each boy was seen privately by the psychologist, who reported later to the board.

Then, in the afternoon, the full board saw each candidate in turn. As each nervous boy came through the door, twelve searching eyes looked him up and down. I recalled my entry at the age of thirteen in 1932 into the forbidding Admiralty Board Room and facing what seemed to me a lot of very ancient men. We tried to put each candidate at his ease but I doubt if we succeeded.

It was interesting work. The ones who did best were those who didn't try to impress and were just themselves without any frills. I always tried to probe and find out if they really wanted to join the service or whether they had some unreasoning romantic idea of life on the ocean waves. Each interviewer had a slightly different agenda and unique way of questioning the candidates. It must have been a tremendous ordeal for them.

As soon as each boy left the room, in turn we each gave our assessment of him and it was fascinating to hear the differing interpretations of his potential. Mostly we agreed, but occasionally we had hot arguments and then the president had the casting vote.

It was a long and intense day and we did not finish till nearly supper time. After supper we had all the candidates' application forms for the following day to read. There was no time to go home during the week, which was disappointing for me after my long absence at sea, but we did have a long weekend from 5.00 pm on Friday until late pm on

Sunday, when we had to be back in time to read the 'crime sheets' of the next lot of applicants.

After a few months to allow my feelings to settle down and talk to Angela after my long time away I finally made up my mind to resign. With a heavy heart I wrote a letter of resignation to my boss to be forwarded through all the 'usual channels' to the Board of Admiralty: 'Sir, I have the honour to submit, regretfully, my reasons for wishing to retire in 1963,' and then I set out my reasons. I was lucky that an old friend who had served with me in *Duke of York*, and who was now the responsible rear admiral, quickly approved my reasons for retiring and forwarded my letter to the Admiralty, who took three months to consider such a weighty matter. In February 1963 I was told: 'Captain McCrum may be informed that Their Lordships have approved that he may be allowed to retire in 1964. He will be informed of a firm date as soon as possible.' That was it. The die was cast. Now I had to find a job.

To try and find out the precise date of my retirement I called on the vice admiral, who actually took the decisions on these matters. I reminded him of my retirement letter and asked if he could give me any more information. He was painfully dismissive.

'You wouldn't have been promoted, anyway.'

Thank you very much, Sir, I thought, but it wasn't the question I had asked. Then he added, 'We'll let you know shortly.'

The Navy used to like to control you. It was for 'them' to decide when you retired and it did not like mere captains taking the initiative. I felt quite miffed by this brusque reception and left his office with a bad smell up my nostrils.

To compound this unhappy reception I was informed that, 'It would not be appropriate for an officer who had decided to leave the service to continue to interview those who wanted to join it.' A fair enough point. I was shunted up to the Ministry of Defence in Whitehall for my final months.

It turned out to be a short but most interesting last appointment. I was to be the chairman of a small committee of communications specialists of all three services whose task was to recommend how to combine the communications systems and staffs of the Admiralty, War

Office and Air Ministry into one integrated organisation in the revamped Ministry of Defence.

It was an interesting experience for my team, which consisted of a wing commander RAF, a lieutenant commander RN and a major, Vivian Edwards, a colleague from NATO days in Norway. Our report recommended some fairly radical surgery on the separate signal staffs of the three ministries, which caused some angst in the Whitehall portals, but it was all obviously necessary. What was called the McCrum Report was approved by the Chief of Defence Staff, Lord Mountbatten, in February 1964, but I had flitted by then, which was convenient as none of the aggrieved officers in the single service ministries could get at me.

To counterbalance the earlier unpleasant encounter with the appointing admiral, Lord Mountbatten wrote me a pleasing farewell letter of congratulations, which I will quote in full as it gave me such a rewarding finale:

> My Dear McCrum,
>
> I have today taken the parts of your sub-committee's report, which deal with the organisation of Signal Staffs in the Ministry of Defence, and I would like to congratulate you on an excellent piece of staff work.
>
> Although I have previously thanked your committee as a whole for its work on the Ministry of Defence communications facilities I recognise that the staff organisation was almost entirely your own work.
>
> Well done and very good luck on your new appointment.
>
> Yours very sincerely
>
> Mountbatten of Burma

SUNSET

On my last day in the office and in the Navy, just before the Christmas break, a few of my colleagues gathered to wish me good fortune over a drink and presented me with a book of poems I had asked for.

Then I walked out of government service for the last time, feeling empty as I crossed Westminster Bridge to catch the Petersfield commuter train. Sitting in the train, watching the mosaics of the countryside flash past, I reflected on my thirty-one years of sea service. From the age of thirteen to this last day, when I was forty-four, I had served king, queen and country. At the beginning, undergoing training at the Royal Naval College, Dartmouth, I had doubts about my choice of career and became a bit of a rebel against many of the absurdities of naval discipline. I was also consumed with anti-war feelings after studying the history of the First World War and reading the war poets such as Sassoon, Owen and Sorley. I wished I could change my career.

On leaving the college I went to sea and my anti-war feelings were soon swept aside as it became clear that we had to face the Nazi evil and I also found that the sea beguiled me. I revelled in the might of the sea, the towering waves in rough weather, the shimmering surface under a calm moonlight and the constantly shifting patterns etched on the face of the sea by wind and clouds. It satisfied something deep inside me, as did the closeness and the friendships of a crew where we all depended on each other. I forgot my doubts and accepted my lot happily.

Came the war years, which, if you survived, was a fantastic experience, exposing every corner of one's character to unexpected trials. Those years gave me much pride in my service.

After the war, to my surprise, I was more successful than I had expected to be. Early promotions gave me rank and interesting jobs and the Navy became my home and my family. I enjoyed the camaraderie that officers and men can enjoy in small ships, the banter, the sentiment, and the sheer fun of being amongst young and exuberant people. Seniority and pomposity arrived in due course as promotion overtook me, but the jobs became even more interesting and challenging.

Now, the final heartrending moments as I realised it was all over, but I was also ready for a new challenge. When I joined the service in 1932 there was a strong sense of national pride in our country and the British Empire, on which the sun never set, and in our worldwide Navy that guarded it. It isn't fashionable now to express pride in an empire that covered a quarter of the globe, but looking back it was no mean feat for a small island in the North Atlantic, to rule over such far-flung and diverse lands.

When I first went to sea there was a naval squadron on every sea on the globe, from the China Seas to the Americas, from the Southern Oceans to the North Atlantic, and in the Mediterranean and Arabian Seas. There was no piracy and maritime peace was preserved. By now, the Empire had virtually disappeared; the Navy was a shadow of its past magnificence and there was a profound mood of self-indulgence and anti-militarism in the country.

The words that I had gazed at high up on the face of the Naval College every morning as the White Ensign was hoisted at the masthead, no longer applied:

ON THE NAVY UNDER THE PROVIDENCE OF GOD THE SAFETY AND WELFARE OF THE COUNTRY DEPEND.

It was time for me to 'abandon ship'.

Index

INDEX